Praise for Being Beautiful

If you've picked up this book because, as the title suggests you are looking for the Beautiful REAL YOU be prepared to find it! An experience more than a read and like a favored walk through a beautiful forest, you will return to 'Being Beautiful' many times to replenish that native hunger in all of us for a sustained sense of well-being. A gentle genius, Tony expertly guides and supports our fragile self-esteem through a journey of revelation until we reach our destination - that innate knowing of who we truly are. Upon arrival we can only celebrate the joy of Connection to Source. To this I say only one thing...bring it on!

Deirdre McGuire - Stress Relief Expert, Life Coach and Master Change Agent. Author - *Can You Believe It!: Ordinary People - Extraordinary Stories* www.deirdremcguire.com

Master storyteller, Tony Cuckson, takes us on the journey of a lifetime in Being Beautiful. He skillfully weaves together ancient lore and modern wisdom to help us awaken to our true selves. Anamcara (Soul Friend) Cuckson guides us ever-so-kindly and patiently toward the light of our being. From beginning to end, readers will feel the author's love and encouragement in true anamcara fashion to go deeper, to let go, to finally see ourselves as we naturally are—by birth and destiny—soul beautiful.

Janice L. Lundy, DMin. Author - *My Deepest Me: A 30-Day Guidebook*. Co-Founder & Co-Director, Spiritual Guidance Training Institute. www.JanLundy.com

This is not just another trendy self-help New Age book to be read and shelved to collect dust. This is a living breathing 'how-to' guide for the contemporary human to lead a fulfilling life guided by spirit, leading with the passion and purpose of the heart. Being Beautiful is a 'call to adventure' to reclaim your God-gifted sovereignty and your birth righted freedom to become who you are! Know that as you bless yourself by applying Being Beautiful teachings into your daily life, you too are blessing countless others.

Michele Gleeson - Integrative Health and Wellness Consultant and Soul Mentor.

Tony Cuckson tells stories with a singular purpose: an invitation to fall in love with who you are, beyond the mask of personality. Tony's book is an invitation to awaken the Sleeping Beauty that lies within you. The happy ever after is, fundamentally, the awakening of beauty. In the repeated mantra, 'you are beautiful', echoed in a hundred stories and poetic metaphors, Tony Cuckson offers a healing to all of us who have been deemed ugly, misshapen or injured by experience. Our bodies and our minds are healed: we become beautiful.

Diarmuid de Faoite - Actor and Drama Therapist

Tony Cuckson has tapped into the deep wisdom that lies hidden in Irish mythology. Through poetry, metaphor, magic and wonder he invites you to realize the wonder tale you are.

John Spillane - Musician, Songwriter, Storyteller, Poet and Dreamer
www.johnspillane.com

Tony's book Being Beautiful is a wonderful tonic for tired souls along the journey. He reminds you of your own beautiful nature and how you can access and live from it. He reminds us we can peel back our layers of armor and treasure who we truly are right now and to live in the now.

Nick Williams, best-selling author of fourteen books including The Work We Were Born To Do www.iamnickwilliams.com

Being Beautiful

LEARNING TO TREASURE THE REAL YOU

Tony Cuckson

The Yeats Experience Academy

Corrogue Dowra, Co. Cavan, Ireland

Copyright © 2018 by Tony Cuckson.

All rights reserved. No part of this publication may be reproduced, distributed or transmitted in any form or by any means, including photocopying, recording, or other electronic or mechanical methods, without the prior written permission of the publisher, except in the case of brief quotations embodied in critical reviews and certain other noncommercial uses permitted by copyright law. For permission requests, write to the publisher, addressed "Attention: Permissions Coordinator," at the address below.

Tony Cuckson

Street Address

Corrogue, Dowra, Co. Cavan, Republic of Ireland HP41 YY24

www.tonycuckson.com

Being Beautiful – Learning to Treasure the REAL YOU

Tony Cuckson. —1st edition.

ISBN 978-0-9957676-2-1

Dedicated to Christine Knickle and Michele Masters

*It was destined that our paths
should cross at The Place of Stones
in the Holy Land of Ireland.*

*Teach only love, for that is
what you are.*

A Course In Miracles

Contents

Contents vii

Preface viii

How to Use this Book 1

Beginning of Learning 4

Levels of the Mind 11

The Way of Ease 27

Listening to the Story 51

Unfolding the Story 59

The Practices 94

The Way of Beauty 127

Conclusion 143

Bibliography 147

Other Books 153

Preface

People of Orphalese,
beauty is life when life unveils her holy face.
But you are life and you are the veil.
Beauty is eternity gazing at itself in a mirror.
But you are eternity and you are the mirror.
- The Prophet - Khalil Gibran

Living as the REAL you leads to authentic happiness, inner beauty, prosperity, true life purpose and to the Grace of Presence. The REAL you is your true story beyond the story of personal limitation you tell yourself from the voice in your head that you think you are. Your real story is that you are a beautiful and unique expression of Love's purpose. You become a revelation of beauty when you learn how to allow your personal story to be in alignment with the Universal story. In alignment with this Universal story you learn that you matter very much. You learn that your contribution to the happiness of all matters. This book invites you to awaken the Sleeping Beauty within you where your real happiness lies. It shares with you the four treasures you are invited to claim so that you can be the treasure you are created to pour into the world. In this way you find true fulfillment. You are blessed and you can bless.

What does it mean to be beautiful? Does it mean having the right kind of face and body, wearing the right clothes and portraying the right image? All these may express a certain culturally determined beauty. This is not what it

Being Beautiful

is to live as one who knows and feels themselves as 'being' beautiful and knows beauty to be an essential quality of who they are.

Authentic beauty is beyond image. It arises from Being. You are made in the image of Divine Presence. This Divine Presence is Love. You are the beautiful creation of Love's imagination. You are also a human being. The word 'human' is 'hu' and 'man.' The word 'hu' means "The sound of Creation." You are thus already a resounding success. You are a unique expression of Creation. When you feel this unique connection you know what authentic beauty feels like. You know yourself, not simply as a beautiful person, but as the Presence of Beauty in form.

Being beautiful is not something you do. It is a revelation of who you are. You can make yourself look more beautiful. There is nothing wrong with making yourself look more "beautiful," however if this is your only connection to "being beautiful" it will not last. To ask, "What does it truly feel like to be beautiful?" will take you on your own unique vision quest and help you in realizing, "Who am I." This in turn will help you realize that you are beauty in form, even if that form you experience as your body is not culturally affirmed as being beautiful.

Let me begin with a definition of Being Beautiful. This definition will be unfolded through storytelling, poetry, lyrics and practices.

> *Being beautiful is knowing who you are as a unique expression of Love flowing through the form of the body willingly open to the emptiness that is forever full.*

This is not the usual definition of beauty you find in the latest beautiful people magazines. Magazines focus is on image, celebrity and personality. The definition given here is on feeling the connection to the Essence you are and finding fulfillment through pouring that Essence into the world to bless yourself and others.

Preface

Being Beautiful requires that you reverse the way in which Western culture has programmed you to feel and act in the world. You move from identification with the mask of personality to the felt beauty of Divine Presence and learn to know who you are beyond the intellect. You are so much more than the information about yourself you present to the world. Like Cinderella you give up rags for riches. You take authority for awakening the Sleeping Beauty within you and live happily ever after because you move beyond time into and experience of the Timeless.

Awakening to Beauty is not something you do. It is more a letting go and letting be. By doing this you will feel encouraged, excited and empowered. You let go of the story that you are other than beautiful and magnificent. You give up identification with the story of the personality or the mask you present to the world to prove you are acceptable so that you might belong. This is the story of the separate self, which is your personal story. This story always has conditions. You think, "If they really knew who I was maybe they wouldn't like me. Maybe no one would truly love me."

Being Beautiful you grow into a paradoxical revelation. You find the emptiness that is forever full. This appears a scary invitation. It is to the ego that thinks emptiness is a nothingness into which it disappears. The ego is correct in its assumption. However, what disappears is your sense of limitation. You open to the Boundlessness of Love. You know true fulfillment through having the courage to be empty. There is no loss here although the ego feels there is and feels threatened by the invitation. This experience is a process you journey into and through. It is a form of dying into life. As mystics from all traditions and none say, "Die before you die so you will know that you are the birthless and deathless One."

The Beautiful People are those who know the real story. The real story of unity rather than the everyday story of personal separation from the One Life. Theirs is the story of unity of the personal with the universal. They know how to live *The Impersonal Life* (1) and create a boundary for the Boundless. These are the people who leave stories pointing the way toward knowing true beauty. These stories are wonder tales that invite you into the wonder of who you are. These are the stories of myth that override the intellect. They speak to you in the language of symbol, metaphor and meaning if you are courageous enough to open your heart to receive their invitation. These stories are maps of the territory that take you out of the ordinary world of the separate sense of self into the extraordinary and boundless world of the true Self. You leave the grey world of Kansas for the colorful and magical world of Oz. You leave the grey world of everyday personal limitation for the magical world of transformation. You take the Red Pill and leave The Matrix.

> *Awakening begins when a man realizes that he is going nowhere and does not know where to go.*
> *~ Georges Gurdjieff*

These mythological stories are treasure maps. They are written in a foreign language, the language of the heart. It is the language of paradox, parable, riddle and mystery. It is the language of non-duality. It is the language of poetry and inspirational songwriting. This is also a language of energy. It moves from the energy of encouragement to Essence. It is a language that invites, not belief, not knowledge but Knowing. It takes you beyond belief. The head does not understand this language of the heart. It thinks it foolish and confusing. The head thinks in opposites. It thinks that either something is one way or another but that it cannot be both at the same time. The heart knows that there is unity to be experienced in opposites.

In this book I share an Irish story entitled *The Four Treasures of the Tuatha De Danaan*. This is both a traditional and non-traditional story. Mythical stories are not set in stone for all time, they change according to the consciousness of the time in which they are told. I tell stories with one essential intention. This is to invite you to fall in love with who you are beyond the mask of personality, so you might know the beauty of living what the mystic writer Joseph Bremer called *The Impersonal Life*. (1) Let me remind you there is no sense of loss here.

Preface

You are invited to expand into infinity (beyond form) and into eternity (beyond time). To invite knowing the Boundless and the Timeless within you surrender the idea of who you think you are and become the knowing of who you truly are. This is beyond intellectual knowledge. You become the knower rather than the one who knows about. Knowledge is information. It can be useful but it is not the felt sense of "Knowing." It is not revelation, it is not insight, it is not insider seeing. Knowing is all of these, as well as the experience of "Being Beautiful." Knowing 'about' the experience of Beauty is not "Knowing" the experience of Being Beautiful. The question the reader is asked to explore is, "Do I really want to be beautiful or do I simply want more information?"

You find the treasure you are by revealing the treasure you are. This is a great paradox that you alone can allow yourself to know. No one can reveal it to you, they can only point the way. To reveal the Beauty you are requires that you become a nobody or a nowhere man or woman. You willingly become as nothing so the boundlessness of NO-THING can flow through you. This is true fulfillment. Nothing is lost. Giving up everything does not mean that you take a vow of poverty. It does not mean you cannot have things that bring you delight. You allow nothing to possess you other than the fullness of the Divine revelation which you then pour away into the world for the highest good of all.

This way of Being Beautiful is a different story. It is the story of Love's eternal becoming. You are a part of this story but never in reality ever apart from it. The oldest story told is of the separate sense of self. In identifying with this story of separation you eat of a poisoned apple that puts you to sleep. You are asleep to your Essence. You are asleep to seeing and living from your true origin and your original face. Mythological stories are pointers to the path of revelation. This path has stages and steps. This path is both unique and common to all those who have walked it. These are the Beautiful People who want you to be the knowing of beauty in form that is Love's Message flowing through an open mind and heart. Will you walk with me now and invite the treasure you are to be known to you and as you? Will you listen a while to the story of *The Four Treasures of the Tuatha De Danaan*.

Being Beautiful

This is an Irish story. It is also a universal story. It is your story. This story ends where you are invited to begin. Begin to know the Beauty that in so many hearts has been driven underground. Fearlessly claim the treasure that Creation knows you to be. Know and radiate the beauty of Being and walk this world Being Beautiful. Be so very well-informed by Love. Let yourself be willing to feel blessed and bless. Let it be so for you. Let it be so for all.

Tony Cuckson Corrogue Dowra Co. Cavan Ireland

How to Use this Book

The best and most beautiful things in the world cannot be seen or even touched - they must be felt with the heart.

- Helen Keller

This book is written with one clear intention. This is to invite you to fall in love and learn to be in love with who you are created to be. In that sense it will, for most people, be a book that invites transformation. This book invites you on a journey. This journey has different stages. These stages are: -

- o The Preparation
    - Levels of the Mind
    - The Way of Ease
- o The Map
    - The Story
- o The Journey
    - The Story Unfolds
    - The Practices
- o The Return
    - The Way of Beauty
    - Conclusion

The best way to use this book will, I think, depend on the reason why you bought it. If your primary interest is in mythology and storytelling then my recommendation is that you begin by listening to and/ or reading the story of

Being Beautiful

The Four Treasures of the Tuatha DeDanaan that is central to this book. Following that you might read the chapter titled The Story Unfolds.

I hope that this will then entice you to begin putting the invitation from the story into practice. You are then invited to choose some practices that you are drawn to. Without practice there is no journey of revelation. Your life, in the words of Dr. Jean Houston writer and principle founder of the Human Potential Movement will be, "The same old same as." If you read the story and the unfolding of the story then it is the hope of this writer that your understanding of the power of story and myth may be transformed or deepened and that you are encouraged to invite that deeper understanding to impact your life.

There will be those who bought the book because they wish to learn to treasure themselves in a very real and empowering way. To experience this kind of transformation needs a radical change of heart and mind. This is not simply changing the content of your mind but more about understanding the structure of your mind. In addition there needs to be an understanding related to your emotional and feeling life. Without understanding your mind and emotions there is no way to experience the power and majesty awaiting revelation from within you.

I recommend that for those who bought the book for this reason that you begin with the chapters that relate to the Levels of the Mind and the Way of Ease. This will prepare you for listening to the story in a way that invites heart awakening rather than head listening. In this way you invite the real power of storytelling that is the transmission of Knowing. This Knowing is not more information or more entertainment but an experience of insight and transformation. It is the revelation that you are beyond compare. You know that you are a unique eternal expression of Love's purpose. In Knowing who you are your life is on purpose. Your life flows and you live as a unique sovereign expression of Love.

For whatever reason you bought this book know that there will be no radical change without practice. Transformation is why you are here. You are

How to Use this Book

here to awaken the Beauty asleep within you. This is the primary reason for your existence and for the manifestation of Creation. Your true happiness lies in feeling in alignment with that primary purpose of existence. This feeling alignment is the most practical way of living in the world. It leads to finding purpose, passion and real prosperity. It benefits you and benefits all.

Finally transformation and the knowing of the REAL you is always an experience of Love and the expansion of Love. It is who you are and ever are. In this book I sometimes refer to the word God. This word has been over used and often misused. I use other words such as Presence, Divine, Infinite and Source. If you find any of these words problematic then please choose a word that speaks to your heart.

The REAL you is a treasure beyond measure. May you Know this to be the truth of who you are, not just as more information, but as a radical experience of direct revelation. It is my wish that this book encourages you to live as that beautiful revelation that Creation forever intends you to be. In this way you will in the words of the Irish poet W. B. Yeats be able to declare, "I am blessed and I can bless." (Vacillation).

CHAPTER 1

Beginning of Learning

Education is not the filling of a pail
But the lighting of a fire.

W. B. Yeats

Learning to be beautiful is a journey in time to a Timeless state that you find you have never left and can never leave. However, you do forget. You become as Sleeping Beauty held in the tower of the intellect. Learning to be beautiful is not the acquisition of more intellectual information. It is letting go into transformation. While it is a journey in time the revelation of beauty can happen in what *A Course in Miracles* (2) refers to as, "the holy instant." This an instant experience of knowing that which is whole and holy within you.

You are always whole, although most of the time this is not your personal experience. Wholeness is not simply the health of the body and mind. It is your feeling experience of union with that which is forever whole. This is the experience of union with the One Life and the One Love. Wholeness is not something you achieve. It is essentially who you are. You have forgotten.

All wisdom teachers teach one thing and invite one thing. This is remembrance. They teach re-union. They teach Yoga in its fullness. This is what your heart and soul long for. Like the Prodigal Son and daughter that each of us are we long to come home to the experience of unconditional Love

The Beginnings of Learning

of which we are a part but never apart from. We are the ultimate adventurers into that dimension were in truth angels fear to tread.

The beginning of learning how to be the revelation of Beauty you are designed to be and express requires a change in your thinking. It is a turning from a focus on the outer world to the inner world. The primary world from which all forms arise is the world of the Formless which is that dimension before manifestation. This primary world is manifested from within. This change in your thinking and focus is the real experience referred to by the word 'conversion.' In writing about conversion I am not speaking about converting from one religious teaching to another. Real conversion is the way in which you focus your attention. This conversion is not a one-time experience. It is an ongoing experience. This conversion begins in all sincerity when you answer YES to the question posited by the modern mystic and father of modern science Albert Einstein when he said, "I think the most important question facing humanity is, Is the universe a friendly place? This is the first and most basic question all people must answer for themselves."

Your inner knowing is your only true compass.
~ Joy Page

This is the beginning of the conversion process that takes you into knowing the REAL YOU. This conversion begins with a commitment to trust your inner knowing. The key ingredient is trust. This is trust, not in another, but in your life force that emanates and radiates through you from the One Life. This is willingness to live from what the writer Penney Peirce refers to as your 'home frequency.' Conversion asks you to make your inner world central to how you live your life. You live from your center and radiate into the world the Light of Love that you are.

This is practical living. You feel connected to the Source of joy. You learn inner knowing, insight and revelation. It is the invitation to another word. This is the word and the experience of 'atonement.' This is the invitation "to be at one with." Your primary purpose is to know and be aligned with Oneness, a willingness to celebrate who you are and know from whom you emanate.

Being beautiful requires a beautiful mind. You already have this. You are a unique expression of the one beautiful mind. This is not the personal mind you think you are that you refer to as, "I, me and mine." This mind tends, for the most part, not to allow you to feel beautiful. This invitation to Beauty is symbolized by the woman in the poem by W. B. Yeats entitled *The Song of the Wandering Aengus*.

> *It had become a glimmering girl*
> *With apple blossoms in her hair*
> *Who called me by my name and ran*
> *And faded through the brightening air.*

The name this glimmering girl calls you by is not your personal name. It is your eternal good vibration. This is the good vibration that calls you home. It allows you to re-member who you are. Once called, you like Wandering Aengus, will search the hollow lands and hilly lands of your inner landscape until you find her again. You stay with her till time is done. The end of time is not the end of the world. It is the ending of the sense of the separate self. The hollows and hills you seek through are not in the physical world. They are states of consciousness you move through in your mind.

This glimmering girl is the voice of Love that calls you in each and every moment in its myriad ways would that you be still and know. This Knowing is different from knowledge. In Knowing you become what is known. You become what you seek. The experience and the experiencer are one. There is Oneness. To be still and know this experience of Oneness is to be still and know you are Love. You know this for certain because the separate sense of the self that is fear filled and doubt filled is no longer your dominant presence. You still function in the normal way but you know you are so much more than you could ever think. You are the Presence of Love in form. Any other information pales into insignificance.

The Beginnings of Learning

Learning to be beautiful you allow Universal Mind to use you for the purpose for which it created you. This is not a mind apart from your own. It is your real mind. Flowing from this Universal Mind is what it truly means "to be in joy of your Self." Joy is the blessing you feel in aligning your purpose with Love's Purpose. Your personal agenda and your purpose is secondary. Paradoxically, however, taking second place to Universal intention allows you to experience ultimate fulfillment.

Happiness is living by inner purpose, not by outer pressures.
~ David Augsberger

The way in which the modern person uses their mind has created a kind of collective insanity as evidenced by the way in which we are destroying the environment on which we depend for our life support. Most people take the voice in their head, that is constantly playing repetitive, tangential fear based mental constructs, as their mind. This is the equivalent of taking a badly tuned radio playing static and white noise and equating it with the sound of a virtuoso playing a Stradivarius violin or cello. One will drive you insane. The other will melt your heart. Mike Scott, singer songwriter with *The Waterboys* calls this mental static "The Madman in the Cave of the Skull. (3)" This constant static in your head is not your real mind. It will never bring you peace of mind. It will never guide you home. It keeps you living in a wasteland of a life lived without ever having known the Love you are.

The first practical step in learning to Be Beautiful is to learn how to unlearn. This is not learning through concepts but through personal direct experience. It is learning how to feel confident in "unknowing." The word 'confidence' means "with faith in." Faith here is akin to the word 'trust.' Trust means you do not know but that you are willing to step into the unknown but not the unknowable. You willingly enter the power of silence in order to be known through.

Being Beautiful

What knows through you is the eternal movement of Love. This energetic movement I call "Knowing." (with a capital 'K') It is not intellectual knowledge. When Knowing happens through you then you will know how beautiful you are. It isn't something you think about. It is a knowledge and intelligence beyond simply 'aboutness.' Knowing about is always second hand. The knower and the knowledge are separate. It might be useful information but it is not information that transforms and takes you into knowing who you are beyond the limitation of form.

We live in an age of information overload. Being Beautiful allows you to move and flow in the Timeless realm of transformation. Your heart longs to feel connected to the Source of Love. The mind you call your own gets in the way. You think you know but for the most part what you know is a "knowing about." Real knowledge, real Knowing is when, out of the stillness of mind and heart, you are willing to be known through. What is known through you is the Message of Love.

This is the way destiny speaks through you and as you. This speaking through you is the revelation invited from the first of *The Four Treasures of The Tuatha de Danaan*. This is The Stone of Destiny which declares the rightful King/Queen of Ireland should that rightful King/Queen sit upon this stone. You are the rightful King/Queen of Ireland but Ireland is not to be simply thought of as the island lying between the British mainland and the United States of America. In the story of *The Four Treasures of the Tuatha de Danaan* the land of Ireland is an inner state that you are invited to know as your Timeless experience of Being.

I am of Ireland,
And the Holy Land of Ireland,
And time runs on,' cried she.
'Come out of charity,
Come dance with me in Ireland

W. B. Yeats

The Beginnings of Learning

You are invited to dance as the personal "I am" unified within that universal I AM state referred to as the Holy Land of Ireland. This is a state of wholeness. It is a state of Timelessness. It is a state where you willingly open your personal mind so that the Universal Mind can know itself through you. Learning how to unlearn, going beyond the personal mind, is a choice you willingly enter. There is no loss here. Infinite possibility and creativity become available to you as symbolized by the fourth treasure that is The Cauldron of Plenty. This Cauldron of Plenty like the human heart connected to the Source is forever empty but forever full. This is true Re-Source-full-ness.

The mind you think you are is the mind of the persona - the mask - the ego - the separate sense of the self. This is needed. This personal mind is a wonder. However, rather than be the blessing of co-creating Heaven on Earth it has become a curse that creates for many people a hell of their own making. We are given free will to create any kind of Heaven or Hell we wish.

> *To understand the immeasurable, the mind must be extraordinarily quiet, still."*
> —Jeddu Krishnamurti

The foundational tool for co-creation is your mind. Change your mind and you change the world. Note here that you are not being invited to practice the power of positive thinking that is simply changing the content of your mind. You are being invited to tune into the One Mind that in reality is the only mind there is. To step into this One Mind is what St. Paul meant when he invited you to put on the Mind of Christ. This is the experience of feeling at one with the Source. This is the Source of Infinite Love.

Putting on the Mind of Christ (Corinthians 2:16 KJV) is not a belief you adopt. It is a radical but most practical way of being in the world. It is the Way of Beauty. Renewing your mind is a daily practice. It invites renewal not only of the mind but the body. Every day give it at least some time. This is the real experience of going on vacation. You vacate the mind you think you are for the One Mind you truly are. You invite the real holiday experience that is a

Being Beautiful

day when you feel whole. In order to invite this experience of universal intelligence flowing through an open mind and heart it is necessary to know about the levels of the mind.

CHAPTER 2

Levels of the Mind

When the higher flows into the lower, it transforms the nature of the lower into that of the higher."

Meister Eckhart

I have written about the levels of the Mind in *Awakening the Heart - 21 Ways to Follow Love's Message.* This is foundational information so I share this information here. This is not a word for word transcript. It is written from the same place but at a different time. This is a manual of the mind that you should have been given so that you can be in Love with the Beloved from whom you are never apart. You learn, not what to think, but how to think. You learn how to use the power of the mind in the service of your highest good and the highest good of all. In this way you learn how to make up your own mind. This is best made up when you feel in alignment with Universal Mind that is in reality the only Mind there is.

While there are levels of mind these levels are not to be thought of as separate. For the most part people access only one level which, in terms of personal transformational power, is the lowest level. Attempts to access other levels of mind are made but they find the way blocked. This is not a punishment. It is simply an energetic law. Many people try to access the higher levels of mind through using drugs. Some do this through engagement in extreme sports. In this way they enter The Zone. The mountain climber disappears into the climbing.

In various wisdom teachings the mind, as distinct from thought, is divided into three levels. You can call these levels different names. In *Awakening the Heart* (4) these levels are mapped as follows:-

> The Conscious Mind
> The Subconscious Mind
> The Superconscious Mind

In this invitation to *Being Beautiful* I will give these three levels the following names and write about them in a slightly different way. These levels are:-

> The Personal Mind
> The Unknowing Mind
> The Knowing Mind.

To become, what the American psychologist Abraham Maslow called a 'self-actualized' human being, you access and allow all three levels. In self-actualization you allow the universal - the Higher Mind - to flow into the body. This is the experience of enlightenment. In Christian terms it is the experience of "Putting on the Mind of Christ." 'The Christ' is not Jesus. The Christ is the experience of direct knowing your connection to Universal Intelligence. It is forever available. It is what you are here to know and be. This Knowing is not a belief. It is your birthright.

Levels of the Mind

THE PERSONAL MIND

Not to be able to stop thinking is a dreadful affliction, but we don't realize this because almost everybody is suffering from it, so it is considered normal. This incessant mental noise prevents you from finding that realm of inner stillness that is inseparable from Being.

- Eckhart Tolle, The Power of Now – A Guide to Spiritual Enlightenment

The personal mind is the conscious mind. This is the mind we use every day. To be more accurate this is the mind that uses us every day. Metaphorically speaking this personal mind is represented by the crowd in the story *The Emperor's New Clothes* by Hans Christian Andersen. This is a story of two tailors who promise an emperor a new suit of clothes they say is invisible to those who are unfit for their positions, stupid, or incompetent. When the emperor parades before his subjects in his new clothes, no one dares to say that they don't see any suit of clothes on him for fear that they will be seen "unfit for their positions, stupid, or incompetent". Finally, a child cries out, "But he isn't wearing anything at all!" This is Direct seeing. It is an aspect of the Higher Mind. It is represented by the innocence of the child who sees and reveals the illusions created by the antics of the personal mind. This collective mind is the crowd who are told what to think.

'Thinking about' has become an obsession. It is the normal addiction of most people. It is for the most part based on fear and separation. It has certain characteristics that are different from other aspects of the mind especially the Knowing Mind. Characteristics of the personal mind include:-

Time based
Distracted
Fearful

Being Beautiful

> Feels incomplete
> Finds life a struggle.

Obsession with the over-thinking mind became pronounced when French philosopher René Descartes (1596 - 1650) declared, "I think therefore I am." This is in fact getting it backward. He would have been more accurate to declare, "I am and therefore I choose at times to think." Since then the obsession with thinking has increased exponentially. This incessant thinking is mirrored. both individually and collectively. in the way we constantly talk and find it increasingly difficult to be with silence.

Personal thinking has helped create the scientific and technological revolution that has given many of us an experience of unparalleled comfort in the history of humanity that would be the envy of Kings and Queens or an earlier era. However, it has lead many of us to think we can think our way into higher states of being. The personal mind is not the mind that can solve the deep problems now facing humanity on a global scale. It is in fact this mind that has created these major problems. As the father of modern science Albert Einstein said, "We cannot solve our problems with the same thinking we used when we created them." We are required, as noted by the German mystic Meister Eckhart, (1260-1328) to move higher and to allow the higher to flow into the lower. We then learn to use the different levels of the mind in service of the One Mind of which we are all an aspect.

The personal mind is time based. It is always old. The personal mind is needed. It just isn't needed to the degree the culture tells you that it is needed. The personal mind is useful for processing information. The personal mind is not transformational. It is very much reactionary and not revelatory. The personal mind is heavily identified with past experience and memory. It is also heavily focused on the future. When I say 'future,' this is the psychological future. The personal mind is needed to plan the holiday but what often happens is that the holiday experience can be made to validate your personal sense of self worth. The holiday becomes an expression of an image you are keen to portray. This is identification with the mask - the persona - the sense of the separate self.

Levels of the Mind

Being Beautiful is not an experience of the personal mind. Feeling beautiful from a cultural identification with what is declared as beautiful is part of the obsession of the personal mind. This is especially true for women in our Western culture as experienced by the vast array of the beautiful people magazines lining the shelves of any supermarket newspaper section. The personal mind is distracted and becoming more distracted with the increasing use of technology. Witness the rise in disorders such as ADD and ADHD. Notice the shortening attention span that is now normal. Anyone who meditates, or has tried to meditate, will know through direct experience that their mind is not their own. You might be in the garden planting a flower bed but your mind is thinking about a comment someone made on Facebook. Before you know where you are you find yourself spiraling down into emotional disturbance.

Your personal mind is like a badly tuned radio. This broadcasts heavy static all day long and for many keeps broadcasting all through the night. This static that most people call thinking is not conscious thinking. It is not creative. It is not thinking that provides solutions to problems. It tends to take you into "The Brer Rabbit and Tar Baby Experience." This is where Brer Rabbit fights the tar baby and with every punch gets himself more and more entangled and stuck.

The personal mind for the most part is fear focused. Witness the individual and collective focus on what is called, "The War on Terror." The war on terror begins in the mind. It begins with the feeling of individual separateness and with this the related idea of limitation. Combine this with the practice of identification with tribalism called nation states and you have a recipe for the disaster that ultimately expresses in some form of violence.

Science has measured that of the fifty thousand and more thoughts that drift through the average personal mind on any day 90%+ are negative. This is due in part, and due in major part, because of the cultural focus on never having enough. This never feeling that one has enough is related to a deeper sense of never _being_ enough. Paradoxically speaking, you can never NOT be enough because you are an expression of the forever enoughness of Love. You can never be enough because you are a unique expression of the Timeless. You cannot ever be enough because the REAL YOU is beyond measure.

Fear is a necessary part of living on this planet. It alerts you to protection of the body. What causes most unnecessary fear is the psychological imaginings of the mind. The ultimate fear is the death of the person that is the mask and not the Essence. This is an existential fear that can only be overcome by dying into life. Fear involves spending a major part of your life trying to find security in what is never secure. You spend time doing your life rather than have Life do you in. When you allow yourself to have Life do you in you find that you are never apart from this One Life. You find that you are eternal. You might at times still be afraid but you know that you are more than the limitation that you identify with as, "I, Me and Mine."

The personal mind suggests that you are in a very real way incomplete. This is true in a paradoxical sense. You are absolutely complete but if you do not feel this absolute as your personal experience then it does not fulfill you. From this revelation of completeness you pour away the overflow. This is affirmed in the words of the Psalm 23:5 (KJV) that says, "My cup runneth over." You can do no other because this pouring away is your real joy. Without feeling centered in this sense of completeness your energetic focus will be on action from lack rather than moving from a sense of free flow. You will always be taking action from doing rather than moving in the world as Love in action.

In the movie _Jerry Maguire_ (1996) Tom Cruise who plays the main character says to Renée Zellweger, "You complete me." As a romantic I love this line but I am not sure I would want a relationship where I had a partner who needed me to complete them. Only conscious awareness off, and living from the Source of Love, can complete anyone. While there is always completion the realization of this completion, as wisdom teachers of all traditions state, is not something the personal mind can attain. It is always given by way of grace. This sense of completion is the last step on the path to enlightenment. You can't do it, it is given to you. When it will be given is not for you to know.

To the personal mind life is very often a struggle. It is the life of do-do. Allied to this always doing your life is your becoming a slave to time. In today's world more and more people experience 'time poverty.' This metaphor of slavery to the personal mind and to time is used in the Bible story about the Flight of the Jews from Egypt. Most people who read the Bible (and probably those who do not) think this is a historical story and take it literally even to the extent that there are people investigating whether or not there ever was a parting of the Red Sea.

The story of The Flight from Egypt is a metaphysical story. It isn't meant to be taken literally. This story is your story, whether or not you are a Christian and whether or not you are an atheist of agnostic. This emphasis on the literal translation of the Bible is what William Blake (1757-1827) the English poet, painter and printmaker meant when he said, "They read their Bibles day and night. Where they read black I read white." Egypt represents your personal mind that enslaves you in time, in fear and in a sense of lack. To be beautiful you have to leave the personal mind to journey into the desert - the unknowing mind. You have to be willing to go it alone. Like the Pharaoh's soldiers your thoughts will follow you looking to continue your enslavement in time and form.

Moses in this story represents the Message of Love as it expresses, and is intended to be expressed through you, would that you trust it to guide you to the Promised Land. Moses is the Knower. The Promised Land is not a physical place but the promise of knowing the experience of wholeness you are and ever are. Once you get to the Promised Land, which is not a place you get to but a revelation you recognize yourself to be, you will know that you never left or can ever leave. You can spend whatever length of time you want in Egypt which symbolizes your personal experience of this dimension of time and space. However, you can never change the primacy of the Timeless.

Being Beautiful

The personal mind, the conscious mind, is a great blessing and a great curse. If it alone is who you think you are the enslavement to the separate sense of self is assured, but not forever. Once you have been to the Promised Land you will want one thing. You will want to return to Egypt to free all your brothers and sisters enslaved in the personal sense of self which is not the REAL YOU. This is the vow of the one who in Buddhism is called the Bodhisattva. This is the enlightened individual who takes what appears to be a strange vow. They vow to stay within the cycle of birth and death in order to save all sentient beings. The last part of the vow declares their knowing of reality. This is, "Recognizing there are no sentient beings to save." The personal and logical mind cannot grasp the magnitude of this understanding nor the magnitude of the Love and compassion being undertaken.

> *The intuitive mind is a sacred gift and the rational mind is a faithful servant. We have created a society that honors the servant and has forgotten the gift.*
> —Albert Einstein

The way to Being Beautiful is not to get rid of the personal mind. You can't do so and it is not recommended. You are invited to expand beyond the limitation of the personal to unify the personal and the universal. You don't stop being you. You are the same and different at the same time. Your sense of 'I am' is allied with the universal 'I AM.' The two have become One but the One knows the two and the two know the One. Your agenda for life becomes, not a personal agenda, but a willingness to be the flow of Love's Purpose. This then lights up your personality from within. This is very different from trying to make yourself a better person. You relax. Your life becomes a do-be-do-be-do rhythm. You become the dance of Love in form. You know the possibility of living from Love in Action. This is both personal and impersonal. There is no sense of loss. There is Love. Love is who you know yourself to be.

Levels of the Mind

THE UNKNOWING MIND

> *"Faith" is not an affirmation of a creed, an intellectual acceptance of God, or believing certain doctrines to be true or orthodox (although those things might well be good). Such intellectual assent does not usually change your heart or your lifestyle.*
>
> *- Richard Rohr, Great Themes of Paul: Life as Participation, disc 9 (Franciscan Media: 2002)*

To realize the beauty you are you have to know the REAL YOU. Knowing is not intellectual. You can study 'about' the real you. You can know all the words but you need to be able to feel the Presence that is the REAL YOU. This is the real source of healing and wholeness. This is a real challenge for the modern Western mind, especially the mind that is the political mind. The Unknowing Mind is the mind willing to commit to a journey into the unknown. You are willing to admit that you do not know and especially that the treasure you seek you have not yet had a glimpse of. This is the case for most people who claim to be believers in some form of religious doctrine. If you once glimpse the beauty of who you are you will know that you could never think 'about' its magnificence.

Many modern personal development teachers encourage you to believe in yourself. Many religious teachers of all faiths invite you to believe in God. Usually this is a God made in their own image. There are billions of believers in God on this planet. Witness the result. Many are at each other's throats. Some will kill those who refuse to believe in their version of the God made in their own image that they have a belief about but do not know. My teacher Jeddu Krishnamurti was once asked by a reporter, "Sir, do you believe in God?" His answer was simple and direct. He replied, "Why the need to believe when you know." Krishnamurti was the teacher whom this writer received the transmission of Knowing from which this book is written.

Being Beautiful

For a long time I have wrestled to understand the word 'belief.' This is as a consequence of my Christian upbringing in Northern Ireland. When people declare their belief in God, it is I think, a belief in the possibility of a God. If they are honest they might admit that they have had no direct experience of the vastness to which this word points. Most belief in God is cerebral. It is simply a choice rather than a revelation. By revelation I do not mean a weekend high gained on some retreat or mission gathering where you claim that you have been saved. Most belief in God is a belief 'about' God. To believe in God is to dwell within the experience that this word points toward. If you have not directly experienced what it is to step beyond time into eternity you have not known what it is to know God. You will thus be tempted to take refuge in a system of belief.

I translate the word 'belief' as, "be life in." The word 'lief' is related to Old English 'lufu' meaning LOVE. (Chambers Dictionary of Etymology) This is a direct personal experience but it is also transpersonal. It is Knowing. Only you can experience and know this. You can only know this by being it. The paradox is that you are already this Knowing but your belief about who you think you are gets in the way. Your personal mind set, your personal identification as the separate sense of self you think you are gets in the way. You lock the door of Heaven which is a state of Being in Love with God.

What if it were declared from every pulpit that only Knower's of God could enter the threshold of living from the vastness of Love? I think the result would be that most religious institutions would close for want of numbers. To know the vastness of that dimension pointed toward by the word God requires that you follow and honour the instruction, "Be still and know." It invites you to be living a life (be-life) within the Presence of the One Life. Notice the word 'in. 'This means that you know you are not separate. You can't be 'in' God and feel separate from God. In being non-separate you are a knower of that which is beyond separation. This knowing is real. You and the knowledge are ONE because you as the experiencer are not separate from the experience. To use the words of the Master Jesus, "The Father and I are one." (John 10-30 KJV)

Levels of the Mind

To live the Beauty you are is beyond belief as a cerebral declaration of acceptance of some holy scripture. The script is only holy to the extent that it becomes the doorway to that which cannot be scripted. When the Master Jesus stated, "Believe also in me." (John 14 KJV) he used the word 'in.' Most Christians have taken this to mean 'believe about me.' This is not what this phrase invites. You are invited to live within the knowing of the Mind of Christ. The Mind of Christ is not to be confused with the personal mind of Jesus. When the Master Jesus says, "Believe in me" he is asking you to have your life lived from the knowing of Christ consciousness.

He isn't asking you to simply believe in the teachings of a historical person. This Mind of Christ is beyond the experience of the personal mind. It is the mind in conscious connection with Universal Mind. This is not something you do but allow to be done through you. You learn how to 'be in the life' that is the knowing of Christ Consciousness. This is a very different journey from being one who is happy to be a believer. You have to be willing to die before you die. You take up your cross and die to the personal sense of self – which is what you identify as you and the voice in your head that is forever playing your story.

The cross is a symbol representing the interconnection of time and the eternal. Jesus died on a cross not to appease some angry God but to lovingly and symbolically show the way to Return to Love. The vertical beam of the cross represents the eternal NOW. The horizontal beam represents time. You are required to die to time - the personal - so that you become the knowing of the eternal and the REAL YOU. The God man symbolically demonstrates the way to Heaven, which is that state of wholeness you are, and is a psychological death into life eternal.

See how much easier it is to simply be a believer. You simply affirm in a cerebral way that the Master did it all for you. Then there is no need to follow the invitation to liberation and revelation. You can simply claim that the Master died for your sins and you are done. The word 'sin' refers to your personal feeling sense of separateness from Love. This is a reality that each and everyone one of us feels living within this dimension of time and space. There is no need to feel guilty about this. It is after all part of the falling upward that is the Return to Love. However, if you still feel separate from Love you have to follow the instructions of the Master Jesus or Master of a tradition that your heart connects to. When I use the word Master I am not being gender specific. You have to be willing to die into Life and Love - to be life in - have your life lived in and as a unique eternal expression of Love.

This requires that you become a seeker rather than a believer. The believer claims to know. The seeker does not know - at least not to begin with. However, the seeker may not be willing to enter the desert of unknowing that is a necessary part of becoming a finder. I have a certain sympathy for teachers of religion. How many people would be attracted to the invitation to die into the unknown? What about the invitation to giving up the personality as your true sense of self? Can you see a market for such teachings? Better maybe to simply claim you know and at least you can then belong to a group and be one of the in-crowd who can claim to know the way home.

In the Bible story of the Flight of the Jews from Egypt personal belief and knowledge about God is equivalent to staying in the land of the Pharaoh. This at least is known. The wisdom teachers of all traditions who know the true way call you into the desert of the unknown with a promise. It is all they have. However, because they radiate the living and loving treasure you seek the invitation is very powerful to those who would be willing to receive it. How many religious teachers do you know who have been to the Promised Land and returned to invite you to give up your enslavement to the personal mind that you think you are? Most religious teachers, in the personal experience of the writer, are themselves enslaved in the separateness of the personal sense of self. They declare a belief in God but do not have their life flowing from the vastness of that word and that invitation.

Moving beyond belief is where the real invitation to Becoming Beautiful begins. It is not a popular beginning. Many simply decide that the slavery of the personal mind is better than taking a chance in the desert. Another way of going beyond belief is to enter what the anonymous Christian mystic writing in the book of the same name refers as *The Cloud of Unknowing*. You are invited to become one who does not know but who is willing to be known through.

This being known through is the invitation from the practical wisdom teaching that invites "Be still and know that I AM God. (Psalm 46-10 KJV) The desert represents the stillness of the mind whereby you are willing to enter the cloud of unknowing. Out of this unknowing you are open to being known through. In this way you have access to the Promised Land of the Universal Mind of which you are a part but never apart from and which designed you in order that it could know itself through you
.

THE KNOWING MIND

> *And I would like you also to come to this innocent ignorance, to this state of not-knowing, because the state of not-knowing – not knowledge, mind you, but knowing.*
>
> – Osho, The Art of Dying – Only the Knower is Left

The Knowing Mind is forever new. It is the source of all creativity. Children live from the Knowing Mind before they are educated to 'know about' life and before they begin to live in their heads in words, concepts and beliefs. They move from living as the flow of the One Life to identification with 'my life.' To be beautiful is to return to being as a little child in an energetic sense and not simply in a biological sense. Like the small child you trust the flow of your energy as being your true guide to Life's direction. You live as a unique dance of Love in form. You live beyond belief. Your mind is empty of any personal agenda other than that necessary to operate in this world of time and space. You are not apathetic. You are not passive. You are powerfully dancing from the power of stillness and silence of No Mind.

Your life is the dance of the masculine and feminine energies within you. In fairy tales the masculine energy is represented by the Prince and the feminine energy by the Princess. They live happily ever after in union because they have moved beyond time which is to say they are not blocked by thought. In effect you choose to go out of your personal mind that is always broadcasting from the Cave of the Skull to be in loving communion expressing from the One Mind. Small children are allowing the thoughts of God or Love to be who they are, which is always who they are and which of course you always are. Except that you have grown up and forgotten how to be in flow.

Our Western education system does not teach us confidence in the paradoxical power of no thought. We think if we do not think about how to solve problems nothing will happen. We are not taught the power of allowing the NO-THING of existence to manifest the needed result in any given moment. Note the use of the word 'needed.' This is different from the word 'wanted' which signifies lack. When you commit to being known through be assured that what you begin to know may not be what you want to know. You may be given to really know that you are created to be a yoga teacher (a teacher of union) when you earn your livelihood as a Pastor in a conservative Christian Church. You might be given to know you are an actor in a family where all the sons for several generations have gone into the military. You might come to know you are a soldier when most all your family members are engaged in peace activism.

In the journey to the Promised Land that is the realization of who you are you can find yourself very alone and feel anything but beautiful. You are required to trust and have faith in what is not yet known but which is being birthed within you. Metaphorically speaking you are tempted to return to Egypt. This is to return to the dominance of your personal mind. At least with your personal mind you know the territory and you can feel you belong with all the other slaves under the yoke of the Pharaoh. The symbol of the Pharaoh represents the power of the collective unconscious which represents the status quo. See how challenging the invitation to Being Beautiful really is?

The Knowing Mind is the universal I AM being known through you as the personal 'I am.' You and the Father are experienced as One which you are forever but which you disconnect from when your personal mind dictates to

Levels of the Mind

the One Mind. This is how most of us live most of the time. We live our lives pushing the river of Life rather than allowing it to flow through us. This is the invitation from the children's nursery rhyme, "Row, row, row your boat gently down the stream. Merrily, merrily, merrily life is but a dream." The dreaming life is the life identified with the personal mind that rows its own way. It is often only through some form of life crises that we begin to ask questions whereby we commit to the quest that is knowing the REAL YOU.

This, I hope, gives you an overview of the holy trinity that is the fullness of the mind of which you are a part but never apart from. This can be taken to be a theory of mind. However, if that is all you take from it then it is simply more information. This information has to be made practical for it to invite transformation. The practices will be shared later in this book. These three levels of mind are not to be thought of as separate. They are 'holons.' They are each a part in their own right but are also a part of a larger whole. Your sense of the REAL YOU is experienced when you are flowing as an expression of the Higher Mind beyond the separate sense of self that is your personal mind. The personal mind is needed to operate within this dimension of time and space.

The next section of this book shares with you how to begin to come into alignment and be in tune with your 'good vibration.' This is learning how to feel in communion with the Source of the One Life that is always in communion with you. What will allow you to be beautiful is to know how to use the fullness of the mind. To be beautiful is to allow yourself to think when you need to think but to know that your true happiness and power is accessed from that state of Being where you are thought through. You are happy to dwell in this state of NO MIND for no reason. However, you will more often than not, metaphorically speaking, return to the slavery of Egypt which is where you allow the Madman in the Cave of the Skull to dominate your energy. In time you will be happy to leave this normal insanity to live in the desert of stillness which gives you true peace of mind. You begin to know the desert is the way to the Promised Land of Knowing who and why you are. You do not then spend time trying to escape or transcend this world. You are willingly available to live as the unique expression of Love in form that you are created to be. In this way you know as the poet W. B. Yeats declares in his poem Vacillation, "I am blessed and I can bless."

CHAPTER 3

The Way of Ease

Ease is a sign of grace in everything – Marty Rubin

Most of us are not living an easy life. Much of this is because we have not been taught now to live in flow. We live our lives for the most part pushing the river. Our culture celebrates the action men and women of the world and not those who are movers from the flow of Love in action. If life is not working for us we are encouraged to do more. We are not instructed in learning how to do nothing and to celebrate the miraculous experience of living from the movement of NO-THING. Doing nothing is not to be equated with the dynamic of the couch potato. Doing nothing is the ability to allow the fullness of NO-THING to do through you.

In Western culture we are not educated in essentials of integral living. These essentials include understanding the structure of our mind, our feelings and emotions. This is like learning how to build a house without using plans. Key to learning to live in, and as beauty, is your relationship to feelings and emotions. Taking command of the madman in the cave of your skull is challenging enough. Being willing to feel into healing is even more challenging.

One of the essential understandings you need to live a fulfilled life is a clear understanding of your emotional and feeling life. Many people use their life energy in the unconscious suppression or repression of painful and unacceptable emotions. I have done this myself. I see many spiritual seekers spend time in what, Robert Augustus Masters, PhD writing in the book of the same name calls *Spiritual Bypassing* (5). This book is subtitled - *When Spirituality Disconnects Us from What Really Matters.* Spiritual Bypassing is where seekers use spiritual practices to bypass painful emotional states. In this way they become more etheric and more disembodied. They spend time trying to get to Heaven rather than embody Heaven on Earth. They become like the character Mr. Duffy in James Joyce's *Dubliners* (6) of whom it is said, "Mr. Duffy lived a short distance from his body." This was the case with my first meditation teacher who taught Vipassana Meditation.

This was the case when Sangharakshita — Founder of the Friends of the Western Buddhist Order (FWBO) first taught meditation to students when he returned to London from having lived in India. He found that students he taught meditation to became more depressed rather than more alive. This was not the experience he had in India. This is because Buddhism emphasizes detachment. Western students particularly loved this idea. They learned how to be detached from emotions they were already detached from. In my experience with followers of the Krishna Consciousness (ISKCON) movement the same thing happens. Within this organization there is strict control of sexual feeling. The Krishna Consciousness devotee is advised that all they have to do to be happy is chant their way out of the material world from which they already feel disembodied.

It is useful here to make a distinction between emotions and feelings. The best way to demonstrate the difference is to use the example of the life of a small child. This child is three years old. It is loved by its parents. It feels, for the most part, safe in the world. The energy of the child flows freely. It feels delight (of the light). It feels excitement. It feels many different things. It is energy in motion. It has not yet learned how to judge one feeling as against another. It will of course learn this. Symbolically speaking the child will eat of the Tree of Good and Evil. It will in this way be thrown out of the Garden of Eden. This happens each and everyone one of us born into this time and space dimension on the earth plane. It is not a punishment as taught by certain religious doctrines. If you didn't leave the Garden you could not fall upward to the knowing of the other Tree in the Garden which is to live the full Knowing of Love.

The young child feels the movement of energy through its body. They are a free bird. They have not yet learned to 'think about' their feelings and put them into different boxes. In this book feelings are energy in motion without judgment attached to them. They are the dance of life moving through a body that you live in. In the words of the poet David Whyte you, "Live in a body in full Presence." The body hasn't yet been armored. It is the vehicle for the free flow of Love's Message uniquely expressing through you.

Emotion as distinct from feeling is also energy in motion. It has one very essential difference. It has a judgment attached to it. It has the label 'good' or 'bad' or 'allowed' or 'not allowed and many graduations in between attached to the feeling. This is what it really means to eat of the fruit of the Tree of Knowledge of Good and Evil. This is not a one-off event that happened to some ancestors in some distant time in history. It is happening to each and every one of us in each and every moment. The child learns the language of good versus bad and they apply this judgment to themselves. In this way they leave the Garden of the Timeless to fall into time and become identified with the personal mind.

Come out of the Circle of Time into the Circle of Love - Rumi

Rather than the child feeling their feelings, which are their inner guidance system, they attach a thought that then disturbs the free flow of energy. They then identify themselves with the feeling which make them 'good' or 'bad' and become guardians of their energy system. As the medical intuitive Caroline Myss PhD states in her YouTube presentation *Why People Don't Heal and How they Can* (www.youtube.com/watch?v=7kGZfZsTYgo) that most people use 70% of their energy in guarding their energetic flow. In this way they create what the Austrian psychoanalyst Wilhelm Reich (1897 - 1957) called "body armor." This is why we experience what is referred to as, "paralysis by analysis." Analysis delves deep into the analytical and logical mind but very often serves to bypass feeling. The author Colin Tipping writing in *Radical Forgiveness: A Revolutionary Five-Stage Process to Heal Relationships - Let Go of Anger and Blame - Find Peace in Any Situation* (7) states clearly, "To heal it you have to feel it." When the Master Jesus declared, "Verily I say unto you, except ye be converted, and become as little children, ye shall not enter into the Kingdom of Heaven." (Matthew 18:3 KJV) he didn't mean you were to regress to being a child. He meant that you were to return to feeling in flow. You learn to feel in communion with the Source beyond judgments and mental concepts about right and wrong.

In the personal experience of this writer many spiritual seekers would do anything rather than feel their feeling. When asked to do so they immediately leap into the Cave of the Skull. There the madman or woman reassures them that all will be OK. There are spiritual teachers who have experienced cognitive enlightenment but who emotionally and sexually abuse their followers. Author Connie Zweig discusses how this religious yearning can go awry in *The Holy Longing, The Hidden Power of Spiritual Yearning.* (8)

Many people engage in positive thinking and use affirmations to try and convince themselves they feel better than they really do. My experience is that affirmations work in a way not intended. They tell you how difficult it really is to change your mind. The answer is to go beyond the personal mind. You learn to go into the feeling so that you can come to the Knowing state whereby you are affirmed by the Universe. This affirmation is always happening. In learning how to Be Beautiful you are invited to feel into healing and into wholeness. To facilitate this journey I have designed an outline that you may consider following. This will allow you to begin to feel your connection to Source and become a true co-creator with Universal intention.

What if you lived your life without judging your feelings? You might think that this would give you license to say and do anything you wish.

This is not the free flow of feeling. This is 'emotional splurging.' With emotional splurging the individual does not consciously choose to express, or not express, the energy moving through them. I know people who pride themselves on their emotionality. However, their free expression of emotions destroys friendships and connectivity. They are proud of their emotional splurging ability. They are not so emotionally repressed but they have no real command of their energy system (Y.E.S) and especially their mind. They are reactionary rather than responsible (ability to respond). There is no gap between thought and emotion whereby they are can make a conscious choice to express the arising emotion or not.

It is important to distinguish between feelings and emotions. Feelings are free of judgment. Emotions have a judgment attached to them. This judgment floods the body with chemical responses which are often outside conscious control. The judgments can either be 'good' or 'bad' but there is always the sense that the individual is guarded. Do this enough times and it becomes 'character armor.' This is where an individual has, for example, become an angry character. Anger has become their immediate energetic reaction to stimulus from the environment either within or without. This is a pattern they have wired into their brain through repetition.

Feelings invite a wider and freer experience of life. This includes the feelings of joy and Love. I refer to these as higher feelings because they are not personal. They come through you from Source energy when you are not living as a blocked energy system. To stop judging your feelings you learn to become aware that you are doing so. You practice being awake. Being Beautiful is a feeling you learn to abide in. It is a process. You learn how to do it by learning how not to do it. It is feeling process rather than a mental process but your personal mind is involved. Broadly speaking you learn how to move into the higher feelings through the surrender of the personal mind to the flow of the Universal mind. This process that I invite you to learn I call *The Way of Ease*.

It is designed as follows:

<u>Personal-</u>
Encouragement
Excitement
Empowerment

<u>Transitional</u>
Ease

<u>Universal</u>
Expectation
Enthusiasm
Essence

This is not simply a linear system. It is not to be thought of as a ladder but more like a figure eight. The figure eight is the number that symbolises infinity. It is a number that contains two circles joined together. There is a boundary wherein the Boundless is contained. You can start anywhere on the figure eight but there is no beginning or end. The figure eight is a representation of the REAL YOU. It is both bound and Boundless. It is both limited and Unlimited. It is limited within time and Unlimited within the Timeless. This is who you really are beyond your limited sense of the separate self.

The Way of Ease

ENCOURAGEMENT

The need to prove who you are will vanish once you know who you are.

— *Danielle Pierre, Just Make It Happen!*

Encouragement derives from the Old French word 'courage' meaning, "the heart's innermost feelings." Here is a very different focus from entering the Cave of the Skull where the madman or woman gets you to tune into myriad distractions and tune out the magnificence of your own resonance.

Being Beautiful needs daily encouragement. In the words of the poet Rumi you need to be prepared to, "Trade logic for bewilderment." You invite what appears at first to be unknowable to be known through you. It helps to have someone encourage you who knows what it is to be in alignment with their own magnificence. It is important that you begin to invite the revelation you are here to be and not simply acquire more information.

Begin by making a commitment to feeling encouraged as part of your everyday experience. You are not trained to feel this way so it will be unfamiliar to many people. In this modern day technological world with all its negative news broadcasting it is easy to feel discouraged. For some this sense of discouragement turns into a character trait and for all too many into a feeling of despondency and despair. Encouragement is not positive thinking. It is exploring by way of direct experience ways in which you change your energy in a positive and uplifting way. How you do this is part of your unique journey. Make it a fun journey.

For myself I find this uplift in poetry, song lyrics and Kirtan (devotional singing). This is how I start the day. My day begins with entry into silence.

Being Beautiful

Then I listen to devotional songs. I may then read a passage from a book that opens the heart. I do not have a radio or television, nor have I had these for more than twenty-five years. I do not start my day with news and talking heads that broadcast fear and discouragement for the world. I encourage myself to be a broadcast of Presence. I will stay with this silence until I feel connected to that which is beyond the sense of the personal. This is a feeling state of emptiness that I trust knows how to fulfill its purpose through me. I have only one responsibility. This is the ability to respond to the Still Small Voice within and create space for it to be felt. What is important here is the intention. Everything begins with intention.

EXCITEMENT

Out of this interior silence a feeling of excitement often arises. I never quite know what to expect. The focus is simply on allowing and waiting without waiting. There is often a subtle level of excitement that appears. This is the movement of creative energy. It is a kind of magic. It is magical non-thinking. The Universe thinks through me. It knows how to manifest what I need and what it wishes to express through me. This practice is invited by the Master Jesus when he advises, "But thou, when thou prayest, enter into thy closet, and when thou hast shut thy door, pray to thy Father which is in secret; and thy Father which seeth in secret shall reward thee openly. (Matthew 6:6 KJV). Please do not take this instruction literally as has happened in some evangelical conventions as shared by the spiritual teacher Bill Donohue in his YouTube presentation *What is Prayer?*

(www.youtube.com/watch?v=QTgacw-KijY)

Do not confuse this Bill Donohue with the William Anthony "Bill" Donohue President of The Catholic League in the United States. They are very different people with very different messages taken from the same tradition. The closet refers to the heart which is where to put your focus. The door you close it the door to the personal mind with its obsession with over thinking. The Father is in the silence which you then allow to yourself to be known through.

This is not formal prayer. There is no petitioning some idea of God outside yourself for a favor or solution to a problem. There is entry into your private room where the Madman in the Cave of the Skull doesn't go. You wait. You don't dictate but you learn to feel excitedly expectant. This a bodily experience and not a mental experience. You are learning to embody the Presence of Love.

It seems strange at first. Maybe it will feel strange for a while. The Madman in the Cave of the Skull will get impatient. Nothing seems to be happening except that the infinite NO-THING that creates all things is being allowed to happen through you. Patience is required. You wait without grasping. You are learning a practice of detachment but not detachment from feelings. It is attachment to thoughts that pull you into emotion and all too often into reactionary living. This is the drama of many people's lives.

> *The universe operates through dynamic exchange... giving and receiving are different aspects of the flow of energy in the universe. and in our willingness to give that which we seek, we keep the abundance of the universe circulating in our lives.*
>
> *~Deepak Chopra*

It takes a while to learn how to tune into the energy that is your internal guidance system. You begin with intention to listen to the Still Small Voice within and then pay attention to how it makes an appearance. More often than not nothing happens during your period of silent allowing. The gift given from within that silence tends to appear later in the day. During the day you pay relaxed attention to the energy flowing through the body. You learn to allow excitement to arise for no reason. You learn to live in expectation that this excitement becomes you. It brings you alive. You are beginning to become the fourth treasure of the Beautiful People. This is the experience of being a Cauldron of Plenty.

The people who do this process naturally are small children who have not yet had their skull occupied by the collective insanity of over-thinking. You can see waves of excitement move through a small child's body that is not yet armored by judgments from the personal mind. Small children do not need encouragement to flow. They are in the flow. We, however, as adults do need this encouragement to allow ourselves to feel excited for no reason. I see these waves of excitement move through my little Zen Master called Sparkle. This is our little black cat with golden eyes and the magical tail.

Within the silence of allowing you are moving away from the dictates of the personal mind to soul awareness. Soul awareness is that feeling connection to the

Source
Of
Unconditional
Love

This is who you really are but you get caught up in over identification with another source called "I, me and mine." This is the source that you place your reliance on. It is the difference between having access to a well and having access to an ocean. You can have both and it is recommended that you do. Each is needed but without the Ocean the re-Sources for optimal living are not available. Without soul connection you are reliant on your personal resourcefulness alone. You live from the Will to Power rather than the Will to Love.

EMPOWERMENT

You are one thing only. You are a Divine Being. An all-powerful Creator. You are a Deity in jeans and a t-shirt, and within you dwells the infinite wisdom of the ages and the sacred creative force of All that is, will be and ever was.

- Anthon St. Maarten, Divine Living: The Essential Guide To Your True Destiny

As you learn to trust the excitement that is the guidance from your feelings you begin to feel empowered. This is a personal sense of empowerment. You begin to have confidence in yourself. This power is not based on self-image but the moment to moment flow of life through the body. You begin to come more alive. Your body is able to hold a greater degree of energetic charge. Your energy system is not so defensive. It begins to become more allowing. There will be resistance to this allowing. The blocks you have placed against feeling certain emotions will begin to release. You become less judgmental.

You are becoming more of an observer than a reactionary. This sense of empowerment is power with rather than power over. It is a power based on surrender and trust rather than control and a sense of separation that tells you that you are more successful, or less successful, than other people. You begin to reap the benefits of trusting the magnificence of the Light inside you. You begin to know and feel your real power. This is the power of attunement to the inner. You become an insider to the Secret of Secrets. This is not the kind of power promoted by the world. This sense of empowerment expands in a paradoxical way. The more you learn to trust your personal empowerment from within the more you let go. You are beginning to move beyond personal empowerment. You are now entering the heart which is the gateway to soul empowerment. This is empowerment from the Source of Unconditional Love.

Self confidence begins to build. You need self confidence to allow yourself to experience real faith. This is faith in the true Self that you are - the REAL YOU. There are many people who attain personal power but they stop there. Power for your own personal use will never fulfill you. It may make you feel comfortable but it will not give your life meaning and purpose. This is because the meaning of your life is found in the experience of unity of the personal within the universal. You are here to gift yourself to the world as an out pouring from the Source of Love through the form that you are.

Personal empowerment becomes a quiet confidence. It is calm and centered. It is moving more and more from a sense of refined feelings that are the response of an energy system less and less judged from the personal mind. Your personal power is really your ability to allow universal power to flow through you. Encouragement, excitement and empowerment are aspects of The Way of Ease related to the sense of the personal self. This is a kind of personal development aspect but is not based on positive thinking and certainly not based on thinking from the Cave of the Skull.

It is based on feeling and flow. It is a learning how to be open to more life. This is what the Master Jesus invited, "I am come that they might have life, and that they might have it more abundantly." (John 10:10 KJV) Abundance is not the accumulation of things. It is the overflow of the One Life that you are willing to allow to flow through you.

It begins to dawn on you that the more you trust this inner knowing arising from silence the more your life begins to flow. You begin to feel at ease. You begin to enter meditative states without doing meditation. You begin to feel happy for no reason. You begin to Love for no reason. This is because your personal mind is out of the way. You are becoming as a little child. You become alert and alive. You focus, not on thinking but on allowing yourself to be thought through. This is miraculous thinking but you are not doing it. You recognize the great grace of living from the invitation, "Thy will be done on earth as it is in Heaven."

The will of the Divine on earth is done within and through the body that you are. Heaven is a state of Being and Presence that you allow to be revealed through you and as you. It is a process of falling in Love and disappearing into Love. What disappears is the idea that you are separate from Love.

EASE

The more you trust and let go the more you begin to cross a major threshold. You are becoming heart-centered. The heart is the doorway into the Temple of Presence. This is the heart that is longing to come home.

You begin to feast on your life in a paradoxical way. You begin to know that you are the banquet. This is you as more than just a personal banquet. You become a channel for the one, who in *The Four Treasures of the Tuatha De Danaan*, I call The Giftgiver. Your sense of being blessed is that you bless others with the radiance of the Presence of Love. You relax. This is not your personal agenda.

Following your acquaintance with a growing sense of personal empowerment you might stop there. Many people do but this will not fulfill your destiny. Metaphorically speaking you are still in the desert. You have yet to cross the Red Sea into the Promised Land where you abide within the Knowing of the Beauty you are. Beauty becomes your sense of Presence. You are lit up from inside.

For many people life is not at all easy. Each day is a struggle. When one issue is solved another arises. They live on the shifting sands of time. Time is a burden. There is no joy in life. It is simply a question of making it through another day or through another night. The Red Sea is a metaphor for the human heart. It is your heart. It is not the physical heart but the metaphysical heart.

This is the crossing point between the personal and the impersonal. It is the crossing point between time and eternity. It is your personal Red Sea. To be able to cross this sea will make your life so much easier. It may take time for that sense of ease to manifest but this is because you are so habituated to struggle, unease and disease. You are entering a different dimension. What causes you struggle for the most part is you're forgetting of your real power. Enter the heart which has depth.

What allows you, metaphorically speaking, to cross the Red Sea is the knowing of the Promised Land. This is not 'knowing about' the Promised Land. It is a glimpse you need only once. If you don't get a glimpse then you need to spend time around a person who has real authority arising from being a Seer and living as a Seer. Such Shining Ones have no personal agenda. They are soul friends. They are not out to save your sins or convert you to the One Way. This One Way tends to be their way. Soul friends, who we refer to in Ireland as Anam Cara's are out to invite you into Presence. They are not interested in you as a believer. They invite you to be one who lives from Knowing and to experience what is beyond belief.

Unease or disease is a pointer to something beyond. It points toward the experience of soul. I define soul as, "Your feeling connection to Source." Notice here the word 'feeling.' This is not another idea. It is not an emotion which is an idea with a feeling attached to it that takes you into the drama of the "I, me and mine" experience of separateness. This might be a good experience but is still your personal experience.

As one of the beautiful people you invite the experience shared by Rumi when he says

> *Out beyond ideas of wrongdoing and right doing,*
> *there is a field. I'll meet you there.*

The Way of Ease

This out beyond gives you access to the universal power that gifts all things through you. You have, however, to take a step that most of us are not willing to take. You learn to follow the teachings of our higher Self. You have to be willing to go where no man or woman has gone before. You learn to trust in an invisible force that you can't see, hear, touch or smell.

You can feel it but you have to begin to trust a dimension that you are not educated to trust but educated to avoid. This is the deep inner silence of the heart. This is the crossing point we all come to. Most of us would rather stay enslaved to the personal mind and try and work it out on our own. Hence the struggle. There is no such thing as peace of mind related to the personal mind. You will never know the peace that passeth understanding if you, metaphorically speaking, do not cross the Red Sea where the constant stream of thought possesses and enslaves you. Most of us prefer slavery to the challenges of dying to the separate sense of self in the desert of unknowing.

This does not mean you will necessarily live a life of comfort or a life absent of challenges. It may mean you enter a challenging life of service and sacred activism. However, this is not done from any idea that you should do so. It is done because you are having it done through you. Your agenda has become Love's agenda.

If you worry about this it is a pointer to the fact that you have lost the connection. Metaphorically speaking, you have returned to Egypt. This happens. You won't abide in the Promised Land unless you are enlightened. For a long time you will return to the edge of the Red Sea and to the land of slavery that is identification with the persona - the mask. It is important that you recognize that this land of promise is potential within you. At least begin to feel encouraged that struggle, pain and heartache are not just all there is. You are so much more would that you follow the process of discovery and revelation. Start by taking responsibility for feeling encouraged each and every day. Make it an adventure. Remember encouragement means, "You are meant to enter the heart." This is the proper use of your personal will. It is the first step on the challenging journey that is The Way of Ease.

Being Beautiful

EXPECTATION

Energetically speaking you are now approaching what in the Old Testament is called the Promised Land. You begin to feel the real Law of Attraction. You are now being drawn rather than being driven. You are beginning to have confidence in the movement of the unknown. Rather than feel afraid you are becoming confidently excited. You are open to miraculous thinking rather than magical thinking. The universe gives you what your soul desires. These are desires that are very different from the desires of the personal mind which to a large degree are dictated by the collective consciousness of the culture you live in.

As New Thought writer Ralph Waldo Trine reminds us, "You are beginning to feel in tune with the infinite." (9) You begin to expect to feel a sense of fulfillment. You begin to relax. Life flows. You are now a true co-creator but your role is not to dictate what you co-create but what you allow to be wonderfully co-created through you. You want less because your inner experience fulfills you. There is no drive to success which is a major pressure in this never enough culture with its focus on never ending economic growth that does anything but cultivate. The real never-ending growth is into the infinity of Love. The focus on economic growth represents the outer manifestation of an inner desire. The culture doesn't value the soul's desire yet these are the only creative forces that last. This is because these NO-THINGS are outside of time. Your sense of expectation becomes focused on how you will serve from the fullness of Being. It is service simply from a sense of fulfillment. I have witnessed the invitation to be of service within various religious groups that I sometimes attend. Such service, however, is usually on condition that you become a member of the group. This is not the kind of service invited from alignment with Love's purpose. The paradox of living in expectancy is that you don't expect much. What you do expect is to become channel of gift giving.

The Way of Ease

Expectation allows you to greet each day as a new opportunity for loving. Rumi says, "The dawn has secrets to tell you. Do not go back to sleep." The sleep Rumi is referring to is the sleep induced by the over-thinking of the personal mind. This is symbolized by the story of Sleeping Beauty in the Tower. The dawn is where you begin to feel the Light. The Secret referred to by Rumi is not the Law of Attraction that involves vision boards and active mental imaging (magical thinking) but the vision of one who is a true servant of Love's Message. This is a vision arising from inner seeing and Knowing. It is said that what you think about all day is what you attract and who you will become. You are advised that all you have to do is change your thoughts and you change your life. However, you are more than your thoughts. What will change your life is changing your mind. This is not the content of your mind but your relationship to the structure of you mind. This is different from focusing on changing your thoughts. You go higher and see the world from a wider and more expansive viewpoint. This is the view of your soul. Using Christian terminology this is called Putting on the Mind of Christ.

The feeling of expectancy is a sign you are allowing the purpose of the universe to evolve through you. This is the real Secret of Secrets. It all boils down to this one choice. Will you allow the purpose of Love, that is the driving force of the universe, be drawn to you and through you? You are not required to know what that purpose is. It happens as and when it happens. You still operate within this world of time and space but there is an underlying aliveness that animates you arising from the Timeless. You are more present because you know the most exciting opportunities come from the flow of the infinite through you. Your mind is still and attentive. You are not planning your life in detail. You are simply feeling in alignment with the eternal plan. This plan is forever fluid. Whether or not this plan will flow depends on you.

Expectation leads to a strange paradox. You begin to become no one special. Your specialness has more to do with your being a channel. The greatest nobody special was the Master Jesus who declared, "I can of my own self do nothing." (John 5:30 KJV). Lines from a classic Beatles song called *Nowhere Man* point to the same liberating experience. You become a nowhere man or woman living in the NOW-HERE. You are going nowhere because you are everywhere. This is not just a play on words. Expectancy signifies that you are changing your relationship to time. You are beginning to have the real time of your life doing nothing and going nowhere. This is a total turnaround in thinking. You have let go and let Love be your guide. This is not simply changing your thoughts which is always dualistic. This is moving beyond thought into the feeling of being thought through which is always exciting for no reason.

With expectancy there is no pushing the river as shared in the beautiful saying by the Japanese poet Basho (1644 - 1694) "Sitting quietly, doing nothing, Spring comes, and the grass grows, by itself." There is no focus on personal achievement. No deadlines so much as there are myriad lifelines. Your task is to learn how to go with the flow but you expect and you get to live from the Ocean of fulfillment of which you are an eternal expression.

ENTHUSIAM

Enthusiasm is experienced when expressing the highest potential within you. This is not a focus on achievement but on wholeness. Enthusiasm is experienced when you are living what *A Course in Miracles* refers to as "the holy instant." What will be achieved through you will be more than you could ever do through willpower alone. Enthusiasm is a sign that your personal will is aligned and subsumed to the Universal Will. "Thy will be done on earth as it is in Heaven@ is an invitation to live from enthusiasm.

The word enthusiasm is defined as follows:-

> *Intense and eager enjoyment, religious fervor supposedly resulting from divine inspiration. From 'entheos' meaning possessed by a God (based on theos - God).*

The Way of Ease

This is more than feeling lukewarm. You become possessed in a positive way. This is a willing possession. You have allowed the *Bright Field* to be your field of awareness. You have allowed *The Long Time Sun* to radiate through you. Many people, especially the young seek ways into this form of delightful possession through using drugs. They look for ecstasy that is experienced as a deep and meaningful feeling connection to Life. Only in using drugs they knock on the back door of Heaven which very often results in a descent into the hell of separateness called addiction.

Enthusiasm is the natural outpouring of the soul. It is the outpouring through you from the eternal Gift Giver. You feel this connection because you are letting go into trust and into the silence of NO-THING that is everything. Enthusiasm is not accessed from the personal mind. You cannot think yourself into enthusiasm. You allow the thinking of the Divine to be thought through you. This is not conceptual thought. It is insight. It is revelatory. It is easy. It is holistic. You know what to do. You do not worry about how it gets done. This is the beginning of the real experience of faith. It is a feeling connection to that which is beyond the known. Emptiness is recognized, energetically speaking, as the open door to fulfillment.

The loss of enthusiasm is a result of being possessed by the rational mind. The rational mind is needed but is deeply out of balance. I have experienced the arising of enthusiasm. many times. Often when I went on retreat to various Friends of the Western Buddhist Order (FWBO) Centers I would walk around the lanes of Wales and Norfolk and find myself feeling happy for no reason. The natural inclination of the personal mind was to want to possess this happy feeling. The result was, as I found to my cost, that wanting to hold unto this feeling ensured its disappearance. It takes practice to not grasp at happiness arising for no reason. The reason it happens is that reason is not primary. Silence and stillness become primary. It seems illogical that the great happiness many people seek comes out of not nothing but NO-THING. This realization is really the beginning of the spiritual life which is the living of the inspired life. This is not your personally inspired life. It is the life lived in the spirit of Love.

Being Beautiful

Enthusiasm is experienced to the degree you trust the universe to be your life expression. You are no longer in absolute control. You never were in absolute control. You give up control to be danced through. You allow the Absolute to lead you in the dance. You willingly follow. The dance is forever new. It can only ever be danced through you. This dance will never happen again in the form that you are. In this dance you get to disappear into the Beloved and the Beloved disappears into you. This is real ecstasy. You won't get this experience using drugs. It is a kind of madness. You have given up logic of bewilderment (Rumi) of unknowing so that you be known through. This divine madness is wildly creative.

> *It's faith in something and enthusiasm for something that makes a life worth living."*
> ~ *Oliver Wendell Holmes*

We crave spiritual ecstasy and mistakenly seek it in material fulfillment. We are encouraged to become possessed by possessions. We want more money, the bigger house, the fancier car. There is nothing wrong in having such possessions provided they do not substitute for Essence. There is now the fashionable focus on the personal development technique called The Law of Attraction or by another name it is called *The Secret*. I call the way in which this law is taught The Law of Distraction. Ecstasy allows you to know the Beauty of the dance of creation you are. You are quietly falling in love with the deepening silence that you are falling into. You hear the voice of stillness speak to you from the deep heart's core.

You do not seek ecstatic experience which tends to be a focus coming from personal self interest. You know that ecstasy is given. Your work is only to get out of the way. You get out of the way for one reason only. Your heart longs to be in union. It longs to serve Love's purpose. You are willing to wait for the Beloved to arrive in the Beloved's own time which will take you outside of time. Then you will really have the time of your life. Rather than experience the insanity of the never-ending demands of the Madman in the Cave of the Skull you become divinely mad. There is no loss here except the idea that Love isn't who you are. This energy is wild. It is wildly creative. When not experienced and expressed creativity it become repressed and wildly destructive through acts of terrorism, street violence, drinking and drugs. Enthusiasm is sensational. It allows you to come to your senses. You sense your belongings. You live from the beauty that is the REAL YOU.

THE WAY OF EASE

This gives you a guide to feeling your way into the beauty that is the REAL YOU. You might not be ready to allow the totality of unconditional Love to be your experience. You might be suspicious of Love's invitation. You might have been wounded by love as many people are. You might feel you are in some way unworthy of this unconditional Love. You are never not worthy but unworthiness is a habit most of us learn. For all too many people unworthiness is their psychological home base.

However unworthy you feel you have the choice in each and every moment. You might not feel that you have much choice but you will have some. You can begin with the practice of finding encouragement. Begin to collect little treasures of encouragement. Make this a daily adventure. Each day choose to look for and feel the energy of encouragement. This is not positive thinking which is always to some degree dualistic and oppositional. It is not practicing affirmations. It is paying attention to how you feel. You are getting out of your head into the awareness of your energy body - your personal Y.E.S.

Focus on knowing what it feels like to be alive from the inside out. What encourages you will be different for different people. It is important you take responsibility and practice. Learn how to feel in tune with your unique resonance. Commit to honoring the unique way in which the universe sings and plays through you. The song you are here to sing, to play, to resonate as a gift to the world is unique to you. Do not that this literally. You do not have to be a singer. Allow the energy to move through you in free flow in the way that allows you to feel enthusiastic for life.

You may not feel enthusiastic. You probably do not feel essential. You might not even feel excited most of the time. View this as a work out, or more to the point, view it as a play-out. You are not so much going to the gym each day. Enter the body temple where you invite the arising of the potential seeded inside you. In this way you commit to "companioning your greatness." You begin to return to feeling your energy body. Many people are scared about feeling their feelings. They would rather think about feeling than feel. They think they might open a personal Pandora's Box.

Start with kindness. Be patient. Learning to feel into and companion your greatness is an art. It requires commitment, practice, patience and at least some little passion. You will fall by the wayside time and time again. The Madman in the Cave of the Skull will call you into separation again and again. Remember however, that there is a way out. Any little step you take to invite the Light to be the light radiating from within you gifts the world the healing it needs. It blesses you and blesses others. You may not see the results but you need to feel the results. Through learning *The Way of Ease* you are learning how to feel alive. You are learning the reality of be-lief. This is not living from the words, labels and concepts you think you are. It is living as a unique expression of the free flow of Y.E.S. Begin with saying Y.E.S. To begin with all you might have is a sense there is more to you than you can 'think about.'

That is the first step in encouragement. Become an artist. Dedicate yourself to being the best you are created to become. This is not simply a focus on achievement. It is a focus on unfolding. It is more a feminine energetic than a masculine energetic. Both are needed. One is the energy of birthing. The other is the energy of manifestation. This is the real invitation to be born again. You are birthed into the revelation of Oneness rather than your continuing identification with separation. Your original birth was being born from Oneness into separateness. Your work is to return to the Oneness of Love.

The Way of Ease

During the writing of this book I am learning to play the keyboard so that I might sing devotional songs from different religious traditions This requires practice each day. It requires meeting resistance and moving out of comfort zones. Sometimes I indulge the resistance but when I practice I find I feel so excited that I simply play on. Time stops. Treasuring the REAL YOU is an art. It is the art of falling in love with who you are created to be. This is a falling upward through the paradoxical descent into letting go. You are learning how to stand in Love. You learn that this Love is an inside job. You stand, not on the shifting sands of time, but on the rock of the Timeless that you are.

Your focus is not on making yourself a better person which is related to self image and what the culture, family and tribe approves off or not. Someone whose focus is on making themselves a better person is not in Love with who they are. They tend to be script writers because the script always has to be better. They are judges of their energy flow. *The Way of Ease* is the way of feeling. It is a way of sensing. You learn to go out of your personal mind into the body. You are here to embody the radiance of Love in form. You are not here to think about how that should be achieved. Love, as the primary driving force of the Universe, is more than able to unfold its purpose through you. Your focus is to trust this magnificent unfolding. The paradox is that when magnificence flows through you it will humble you. You will know one thing for certain. You could never deserve the power and the beauty you are given unconditionally from the Giftgiver. You will want everyone to enjoy, and be in joy of, this gift.

Your happiness will increase to the extent you learn how to be thought through. This gives rise to happiness for no reason. It arises out of silence and non-doing. Life becomes you being done through. You are in flow. You worry less. You recognize that worry is a sign that suggests you are in complete control. This is the idea that the personal mind is in control of the Universal Mind. Happiness is when the personal mind and the Universal Mind are one.

The Way of Ease is less doing and more allowing. You begin to explore the experience of Y.E.S and learn how the Universe says Y.E.S through you. Happiness for no reason is a sign. Excitement around creativity is a sign.

Being Beautiful

Expectation is a sign you are truly aligned with the Law of Attraction. You become attractive in the real meaning of that word. You are falling in Love with who you are created to be. Things are falling into place from the no place you would rather be. You are going nowhere and getting everywhere. You are morphing into the paradoxically multidimensional miraculous thinking individual you are. You are realizing the beauty and power of the REAL you.

You give up the old story of the personal for the living revelation of Essence. You return to knowing yourself as one of the beautiful people. You recognize the treasure you are given to share with the world. The more you give the more you get but this getting isn't from wanting. It is a natural consequence of being in love with who you are. You become aligned with Universal Love which simply pours itself away into myriad forms for its own delight. You are one of the Beautiful People. You are here to be one of The Shining Ones. This is the great gift of being born into the leading edge of consciousness on this planet. This book is centered around a story entitled *The Four Treasures of the Tuatha de Danaan*. Let this story be your story which it is. Let this story begin to reveal the beauty you are.

CHAPTER 4
THE STORY

Listening to the Story

A time will come when we realize that stories choose us to bring them into being for the profound needs of humanity.

Ben Okri – The Joy of Storytelling – A Way of Being Free

The story of *The Four Treasures of the Tuatha De Danaan* is told and unfolded with one intention. This is to invite you to fall in love with yourself - the REAL YOU. The story is told in words to take you into an experience beyond words. Many of you may never have experienced that placeless place within where you know for certain that who you are is beautiful beyond measure. This beauty is not something you earn. You could never earn it because it has no measure. You can't get it. You can only allow it to be revealed. This story and how it unfolds shares ways in which this revelation of your true Self can be invited to be your revelation.

When listening to this story of *The Four Treasures of the Tuatha de Danaan* I ask that you reverence this magnificent revelation within you. Make it your intention to companion your greatness. I ask that you reverence the wholeness within and invite the experience of the holy to be your experience. Do not simply make listening to this story just one more piece of entertainment. Let it be an invitation to a new way of being in the world. Let it be a doorway to the treasure you are here to know and to share.

Being Beautiful

For a little while take time and make the time with this story and this storyteller sacred. Make it time whereby you invite the magic of the Timeless to be known through you. To do so you are asked to set aside the necessary time to avail of the gift. You are the gift. This gift is from the Beloved of who you are a part but never apart from. You are required to give its receipt the time and attention that it needs and deserves.

Fairy tales and mythological stories are told with a different kind of language. They are magical. They are mythic and paradoxical. They are riddles and parables. The logical mind tries to analyze and reduce this kind of story to something that it can understand. The Master Osho referred to this as 'logic chopping.' Rumi talks about the same issue when he advises, "Trade logic for bewilderment."

For hundreds of thousands of years the way we learned to negotiate our way through this world was through storytelling. In Ireland the person second only to the King or Queen was the poet and storyteller. Energetically speaking this hierarchy is representative of the higher energy centers of the body that are the throat, (storyteller) brow (poet) and crown (King/Queen) chakras.

In storytelling there is the storytelling trance. This is where the storytellers voice takes the audience into a deep state of listening. In the room you can hear a pin drop. The storyteller gets out of the way and the story is told through him or her. This happens with music and dance. The musician and the dancer disappear into the music and into the dance. The story, the music and the dance are expressed through a performer who has disappeared in the sense that they are no longer doing the actions.

From the voice of the storyteller there can be a transmission of Knowing. You can know what it is you didn't know before. You come home to an aspect of yourself that you had forgotten. This is not more information about yourself but the knowing of who and why you are. In listening to this story you invite listening to your true self.

The Story

The Four Treasures of the Tuatha De Danaan is not simply an old Irish story. As you will discover this story is your story. It is the story of your family. It is the story of the people you love and do not love. The story ends where you are asked to begin. You are asked to go on a treasure hunt so that you may reclaim the treasure you are. This is a quest that takes courage, commitment discipline, practice and patience. You become a disciple of Love's purpose as it created you to uniquely express through you and as you.

Listen to this recording in a quiet space where you are confident you will not be disturbed. Preferably listen while lying down on a comfortable bed or settee. Do not worry if you go to sleep. In the words of the poet Mary Oliver from her poem *Wild Geese*, "You only have to allow the soft animal of your body to love what it loves." If the body needs sleep allow it to sleep.

If you have a mobile phone switch it off or put it in a room as far away as possible and have it switched off. By doing this you are symbolically saying that you are prepared to be in communion rather than in communication. Make the room as dark as possible and if it is safe to do so light a candle to symbolize the invitation to being the light you are here to share. This was the way we used to connect in community around the fire and the hearth. The darkness is symbolic of birthing. This is womb time. It is time to be receptive. You are inviting the stillness that speaks from the real Stone of Destiny to speak through you but not in words.

Listen to the story. After listening turn over on your right side and rest for a while. Your personal mind will begin to kick in. Come back to your breathing. If nothing happens do not worry. Simply trust the silence and the intention. You are stepping out on a new journey and a new story which is your real story. The territory is new and as yet unfamiliar. Do not be afraid of not knowing. Trust the stillness. Trust the silence. Trust the NO-THING-NESS.

I recommend that you buy yourself a journal or notebook to record whatever thoughts and feelings arise from listening to the story or when you read about the unfolding of this story. This is important because it embodies what has been gifted to you from your listening and your intention. In this way you manifest into form that which is arising through you from the formless. In this way you honor what is given from the Giftgiver. You participate in co-creating with the Divine. In this way you honor your personal Y.E.S. that is the Still Small Voice within. You begin to take responsibility for listening to and feeling into the magnificence that speaks through you.

Following your listening to this story do not immediately leap into activity. Give yourself time to come back into the world of time and thought. The intention is that you learn to be in the world in a different way. You are learning to be an embodiment of radiance. Being the radiance of Love is form is the REAL YOU. This is not just more information. It is revelation that revolutionizes your life. It is the Ugly Duckling finally recognizing the beauty and grace of who he really is at the lake of revelation.

I have made the *The Four Treasures of the Tuatha De Danaan* story available for download at the following url and webpage. You can simply read the story but it will be more powerful if you relax, listen and receive the words that point beyond the words. Download the audio recording here.

http://tonycuckson.com/four-treasures-tuatha-de-danaan/

THE STORY

Once upon a time before time ever was there was a people.

My people. The people I love.

They are called by different names. They are called The Beautiful People. They are called The Shining Ones. They are called The Tuatha De Danaan.

They are the children of the Goddess Danu. The one they call The Giftgiver.

The Story

The One who gives her name to magnificence that is the river Danube in the land of People of the Black Eagle.

She gives her name to the river Don in the land of the People of the Bear.

She is the one who gives gifts to her children without conditions.

The Beautiful People, the people I love, lived at a place beyond place in a time beyond time.

They lived in four island cities.

There was the city of Falias. There was the city of Gorias the city of Murias and the city of Finias.

And so it was that as in all good stories the Shining Ones might have lived happily ever after.

Except that they did not.

It happened one day. It always happens on one day.

No one is quite sure why it ever happened. Only that it did happen.

My people, the people I love began to become possessed.

Slowly, they began to claim all the gifts they were given without conditions as their own.

Soon all the gifts received from the Giftgiver where "my gifts."

Then a strange thing happened that had never happened before. A feeling arose in the land of the beautiful people that had never been felt before.

Being Beautiful

They give this strangest of feelings a name. They called it 'fear.'

Soon the feeling of fear was the feeling that began to possess all the people.

But not all the children of the Goddess Danu became possessed.

Yet they knew that if they stayed in the four island cities that possession would take hold of them.

So in boats of silver and gold those who still felt themselves to be Children of the Goddess Danu set sail.

They left the four island cities of Falias, Gorias, Murias and Finias.

They left with the four treasures of the Tuatha De Danaan and sailed into the unknown.

They took with them the magical treasures that are the Stone of Destiny, the Sword of Nuada, the Spear of Lugh and the Cauldron of Plenty.

For a long time they sailed the vast open sea until one day they arrived on a different shore.

They arrived on an island that would later be named by the first poet of this island. This was the poet Amergin. He would give this island land the name of Erin.

Those beautiful people intent on remaining connected to the Giftgiver pulled their boats of silver and gold unto this new shore. This was the shore called Time.

They burned their boats of silver and gold. For three days and three nights the land was darker than dark.

The Story

The people of this island land of time called the Fir Bolg - the People of the Baggage were sore afraid.

After three days and three nights the light returned and the Fir Bolg looked upon the new arrivals who were the Shining Ones.

And so it was that in this new land, the land of Erin on the shore of time that the Beautiful People who left the four islands might have lived happily ever after.

Except that they did not.

In the land of time, on the island of Erin obsession moved more deeply into possession and into opposition.

In this new place, in this very different place the Beautiful People learned a new language and a new way of being in the world.

They give this new experience a name. The name was 'war.' Except that obsession, possession and separation was no longer new in the land of time.

The treasures of the Beautiful People would no longer be instruments of abundance and gift giving. They would be instruments of division and destruction used at the Battles of Moytura between the other peoples in the land of Erin. The Fir Bolg and the Fomorians.

In time the Beautiful People lost the final Battle of Moytura and were driven to live underground in the green isle of Erin.

There, it is told they remain. They remain with their four treasures. The Stone of Destiny, the Sword of Nuada, the Spear of Lugh and the Cauldron of Plenty.

It is told that this is an old Irish story. A story of a time long ago.

Being Beautiful

It is, however, a story beyond time. It is always your story. The treasures of the Tuatha de Danaan are inside you.

The Secret of Secrets is inside you.

The Battle of Moytura is going on inside your head.

Your real story is the story of bringing beauty into the world of time from the world of the Timeless.

Your story is the unique gifting of the treasure you already are.

Your story is the knowing of the REAL YOU by reclaiming your sovereign state and pouring yourself away from the eternal emptiness that is forever full.

In this way, as in all good fairy tales you will then know what it is to live happily ever after.

Let it be so for you.

Let it be so for all.

Audio Recording available here

http://tonycuckson.com/four-treasures-tuatha-de-danaan/

CHAPTER 5

Unfolding the Story

Modern storytellers are the descendants of an immense and ancient community of holy people, troubadours, bards, griots, cantadoras, cantors, travelling poets, bums, hags and crazy people.

-Clarissa Pinkola Estés

The story of the Tuatha De Danaan is told in order to remind you that this is your REAL Story. You are always one of the Beautiful People, not as a time bound personality but as a unique expression of Presence radiating into the form you are from that dimension beyond time and space. This story will now be unfolded in a practical way. You are invited to make a commitment to unfolding the magnificence you are created to realize and gift the world. You commit to fall in love with who you are. This is foundational to living and loving your life as a unique expression of Love in form.

Give this story your attention and invite its deeper meaning to be revealed to you and through you. This is the invitation to a journey of insight and revelation. It makes you a true insider. Commit to taking the next step in exploring what this story means for you. The energy will build if you honour this invitation. You will be affirming to your subconscious mind that you are sincere in learning how to reveal the treasure that is the REAL YOU. Have fun with this. Let it move you from being driven to being drawn. Let it allow you to experience attractiveness rather than distraction. Remember there will be resistance. There is no birthing the new without resistance. The child resists the mother's body. The seed resists the earth. Practice patience and kindness with yourself.

As you read the unfolding of this story allow a line to speak to you. In this way you practice reflection. Do not think about the words but allow the feeling to be known to you. Simply be silent. Relax into allowing revelation to come. Don't push the river. Don't go pulling up the seed so that you might find if it is growing in the way you think it should be growing. Simply let it be.

Letting it be is a practice of not knowing. For most people it will be a new way of inviting learning. You are inviting Creation to create through you. You are practicing trust. You are, metaphorically speaking, in the desert. You have left the land of slavery which is the constant pushing of your rational mind. Pay attention to what excites you during your day. Pay attention to how the Universe is communicating with you. Do not dismiss coincidence or synchronicity. Let us now unfold this story.

DAY 01

ONCE UPON A TIME

All good fairy stories start with the line, "Once upon a time." As a child many of us would feel excited with anticipation when we heard this line. We want to feel a little scared but we also want a happily ever after ending. These stories reveal truths about the journey of becoming a fully realised human being on this glorious planet earth.

Once upon a time sets the scene. The story begins with the word 'Once.' This is related to the word 'One.' This invites connection to the One that is the One Life and the One Love. At the beginning of the story you enter a dimension that is separate from that dimension of Oneness from which you, in reality, are never separate. This dimension is the dimension of time.

Unfolding The Story

Time is brought about by the idea and feeling of separateness. The One becomes the two in order that it can know itself as Love. The One creates the 'not one' to be this revelation. You are that creation. The One is never not One. It, however, becomes separate so that it can know itself as Love. It can know itself both as One and as not one at the same time. It can be the play of the Timeless within the limitation of time. It can be the play of the formless within form. To do so there has to be a forgetting of the REAL YOU so that you can return to Love but with a deeper knowing of who you are.

The primary dimension is that of the Timeless. Timelessness is the same as eternity. The personal mind cannot know the Timeless. From its standpoint eternity is thought to be a very long time that is beyond measure. In Christian teachings the believer is promised eternal life. Usually this is the idea that you personally will live forever in some form of the body in a place called Heaven where angels play harps. You would probably be bored out of your skull within the week.

Most people are enslaved in time which is the secondary dimension. Time isn't existentially real but it appears real to the logical mind. The only time there ever is, and ever will be, is the eternal NOW. Eternity is not a long time. It is outside of time. You know eternity when time disappears. This is the true meaning of the Biblical reference to the end of the world. The world does not end. Time ends. When the world ends you will still know you live in time because you are embodied but you have realized your multidimensionality. You are in the world but not of the world.

To treasure the REAL YOU is to know who you are as the dance of the Timeless within time and the dance of the Formless within form. This assures you that you are beautiful. This beauty is beyond measure. It is incomparable. It is your Essence and you pour this into time as the radiant Presence of Love.

Being Beautiful

DAY NO 2

THE PEOPLE I LOVE

The story of *The Four Treasures of the Tuatha De Danaan* introduces you to 'my people.' These are the people I love. These people are in love with themselves but not in an egotistical way. They know who they are. They know how to be in the world of time while connected to the world beyond time. The Beautiful People are not living up to some mental image of beauty in form. They are not chasing some ideal of beauty. They are not perfect people. They are willing to fully allow their imperfection to be part of the whole they know themselves to be.

> *The thing that is really hard, and really amazing, is giving up on being perfect and beginning the work of becoming yourself.* - Anna Quindlen

They have nothing to prove to themselves. They are clear about their Primary Intention. This is to feel in alignment with the Purpose of Love. Being in alignment with Love's Purpose gives them clear direction and provides them with clear focus. There is less anxiety about what to do with one's life. Beautiful People love for no reason. They are happy to go out of their personal minds to invite the joy of the One Mind to express through them. Love is a paradoxical stand alone experience coming from the ability to stand as a unique expression of the All One.

Most people are never introduced to the possibility that this is how magnificent they are. For most people love is something that happens between two people. It is a subject/object relationship. This can be a very beautiful experience. For many, however, love becomes a relationship of co-dependence rather than a union of radiant inter-dependence and freedom. Beautiful people do not stop loving people or things. The difference is that Love is not dependent on people or things such as job, cars, clothes and houses. Beautiful people source Love from the emptiness that is forever full. This is symbolized by the fourth treasure of the Tuatha De Danaan that is The Cauldron of Plenty. They keep their hearts and minds open so Creation can gift the beauty of the Timeless through them. They are like flutes waiting of the Divine to play a unique song through them.

> *The flute is totally empty. It is the breath that flows through, sings and dances. To be empty is not emptiness. - Rumi*

Beautiful people, the people I love, know Love is who they are. Love is not some THING you create. You are Love created from NO-THING. You are made in the image of God or Source energy. That Source energy is Love. Please note that this does not mean Source is Loving. There is no duality here. With loving there can be non-loving. Loving can be dependent. It can be conditional. It can move from one end of the spectrum to the other.

God is Love (1 John 4:8 KJV). You don't get it. You allow it to be known through you as your direct experience. In this way you know Love as who you are. You are whole because there are no opposites. In the hearts of Beautiful People the sun of Love shines from the clear blue sky of NO-THING-NESS. This is the sky of the One Mind unclouded by thoughts and emotions that are the drama of many people's lives. These clouds of negative habits, ego and fear blot out the sun of Love. The only alternative left is to source love from outside the heart and mind through objects beyond oneself including other people.

Beautiful People are tuning forks for Love. They tune to Source. This takes practice and commitment. When you are standing within their good vibration you feel good. Beautiful People are tuned to LoveFM. They are broadcasters, not of fear and separateness, but of Love and unity. In this way you can receive an energetic transmission from them. If you spend time around such people you too can tune into the wavelength and recognize what it feels to be Beautiful. You will be in Love. You will be a standalone All One good vibration. You know Love is who you are.

Being Beautiful

DAY NO 3

WHAT'S IN A NAME?

In this story *The Four Treasures of Ireland* the people central to the story have many names. They are called The Shining Ones. They are called The Beautiful People. They are called The People of the Shining Brow. They are the Tuatha de Danann - the children of the Goddess Danu - the one called The Giftgiver.

These are not just names. They are resonances. In the era of the 1960's they were referred as 'good vibrations.' To know yourself as one of the Shining Ones you are required to get on this good vibration wavelength. The wavelength is not to be considered good in a simply moralistic sense. You commit to learning how to feel fine. You do this by committing to breathing in a conscious way. The expression "feeling fine" comes from the experience of refined breathing.

Refined breathing takes you out of the over-thinking mind where you are tuned into your never quite good enough personal vibration. This is the vibration broadcast by the personal mind and it is reflected back into the world as our daily news broadcasts. Beautiful people (not to be equated with glamorous people) have a certain vibration. In the words of the American philosopher, mystic and teacher Ralph Waldo Trine they are, "In Tune with the Infinite." They are not broadcasting separateness but unity.

This good vibration mindset is invited by Master Jesus when he said, "For where two or three are gathered together in my name, there am I in the midst of them." (Matthew 18:20 KJV) This doesn't mean three people gathered together in a group bearing his name. It means two or three people gathered together who consciously enter his vibration. In the poem *Song of the Wandering Aengus* by W. B. Yeats Angus meets with a shape shifting woman who calls him by his name and then runs into the ether.

Unfolding The Story

Song of Wandering Aengus

I went out to the hazel wood,
Because a fire was in my head,
And cut and peeled a hazel wand,
And hooked a berry to a thread;
And when white moths were on the wing,
And moth-like stars were flickering out,
I dropped the berry in a stream
And caught a little silver trout
.

When I had laid it on the floor
I went to blow the fire a-flame,
But something rustled on the floor,
And someone called me by my name:
It had become a glimmering girl
With apple blossom in her hair
Who called me by my name and ran
And faded through the brightening air.

Though I am old with wandering
Through hollow lands and hilly lands,
I will find out where she has gone,
And kiss her lips and take her hands;
And walk among long dappled grass,
And pluck till time and times are done,
The silver apples of the moon,
The golden apples of the sun.

W. B. Yeats

Someone calling you by your name, that is your unique good vibration, invites a you to receive a transmission of Knowing. They invite remembrance and revelation. When you are given this revelation, which you will know once you receive it, you will have this transmission go from you. This is because you want to own it. It will change you. You know the REAL you beyond any measure of cultural beauty. Like Wandering Aengus you will seek to re-experience the calling of YOUR name. You follow the Call to Adventure into the wonderland of your own magnificence and companion your greatness. This is the Universe affirming you. It is calling you by the name it gave to you beyond time and space saying, "You are beautiful to me." If you are true to this calling you will find out where it has gone.

DAY 4

THE SHINING ONES

All is light. You are a unique expression of this One Light. You are a unique radiance of Love expressing through the form of the human body. Our individual and collective sense of separateness from this creative Light of Love is the major reason for most unnecessary suffering and violence in this world of time and space. This Shining experience is experienced as lightness of embodiment. You delight in creatively expressing who you are. You shine into the world the light (delight) that lights the way home. This is your true heart's desire. Leading people to delight (to the light) in themselves becomes your delight.

The Shining One's are called, "The People of the Shining Brow." The shining brow symbolizes the capacity to see beyond the appearance of separate things. The Shining One sees from a placeless place of unity out of which all forms arise and return. This is the placeless place of the Unmanifest. In the movie *Avatar* (2009) the people of the planet Pandora affirm this seeing when they say, "I see you." The personal mind hasn't the capacity for this seeing. The essence of the individual is seen beyond the personality.

We spend the day living from the experience of the separate sense of the personal self. For many this is less than a delightful experience. Many soothe this sense of separation from Love through some form of addiction. As a result they fall increasingly into a place of darkness. Western culture invites addictive behaviour. This includes addiction to technology and communication rather than communion. There is addiction to broadcasting fear rather than radiating the light of Presence. Our primary addiction is attachment to our over thinking mind.

The Shining One broadcasts delight. This Light does not belong to them. It comes through them. The Shining One radiates the Light of the World beyond time and space and expresses the message of Love in the unique way intended. This broadcast is clear. Obsessive over thinking gets in the way of this clear broadcasting and rather than experience the Shining brow a furrowed brow is the result.

DAY 05

THE GIFTGIVER

The metaphor of the Giftgiver is the reality behind the manifestation of Creation. It is very different from the story of Creation told me when I was a child growing up in my homeland of Northern Ireland. Mine was the story of a Creator who tempts his children and then punishes them by throwing them out of the home they Love. This Creator then demands that one of his most loving children be murdered in order that he, the Creator might feel better about having been disobeyed. Then and only then can his exiled children return home. If this story were told about any other father it would be called child abuse and the Creator would be referred to the relevant department of social services.

The issue for each of us is our willingness to receive the gifts asked for. You don't earn the gifts given. You learn to allow them to be given through you. This is really an issue of faith. Faith is not to be confused with cerebral belief. If you had faith only the size of a mustard seed then you could say to the mountain move and it would move. Most of us do not have that kind of confidence in receiving what is asked for from the infinite creative force that is Love. It isn't our experience. It isn't how we feel or how we allow the power of the universe to feel through us and manifest the miraculous. Faith is not faith in a dogma but in the feeling connection beyond that which is known. Gifts are pouring your way everyday would you leave the Cave of the Skull and return to allowing Universal Mind to express through you.

To be willing to receive these gifts from the unconditional Giftgiver you open to the soul. In this book your soul is not a thing. It is a subtle energetic which is your personal attunement with the Divine. This connection is never lost but your idea of yourself as separate from the Source overrides this felt connection to universal unconditional Love. Your ability to receive gifts unconditionally depends on where you place your intention and attention. Is your intention to willingly feel in alignment with the Giftgiver or are you intent on creating the life you have separate from the Source of Love which is what it means to build treasure on earth.

You can have both but having treasure on earth is not your primary intent. What is primary is being a treasure on the earth. Your focus becomes one of being a co-creator. Your intent is on bringing Heaven to Earth. This is the radiance you shine into the world. It isn't a question of how you then do your life. It becomes a personal quest to learn how to have Life do through you. You become a Giftgiver of Presence. See how magnificent you really are intended to be? The only thing you need to do is give up the obsession that is your personal mind always tuned out from Source energy and take a leap of faith into the unknown but not the unknowable.

DAY NO 6

WHAT'S IN A NAME

Many of us become possessed by possessions. No matter what we have it is never enough. This is a major part of our cultural focus with its primary obsession with higher economic growth. This obsession with higher economic growth is responsible for destroying the planet and contributes to lower levels of personal happiness.

We are experiencing greater levels of addiction. Witness the everyday addiction to the mobile phone caused by the latest anxiety called F.O.M.O. This is the "Fear of Missing Out." I have friends who listen with one ear to me and another ear to the possibility that someone might contact them on their mobile phone. We wonder why we feel so lonely in a world where there has never been more ability to communicate. We know we are not being listened to. Our conversation between the one we are with is less important than the conversation we might have with someone else.

Our primary obsession is with the personal mind. Most people do not know their own mind. It is like a monkey on a string. They do not choose to use it. It is always using them. The result is the way in which we view the world. There are wisdom teachers who say, "Change your thoughts and you will change your world." Or, "What you think you become." Most people cannot change their mind because they are trying to change thoughts with other thoughts.

They are still possessed by the personal mind. Hence the absence of success with positive thinking, affirmations and the Law of Attraction. To change your world you need to change your mind. This is not the content of your mind but your awareness of the structure of your mind. To use a Christian term you learn how to put on the Mind of Christ. To use a Buddhist term you return to your Buddha nature. This undoes your obsession and possession of the personal sense of self. You become unified with the True Self. No possession only union. There is only Knowing.

Possessions become things you use. You do not allow them to use you. You enjoy them but they do not define the reality of who you are. They are forms through which the play of the Divine expresses through you. Your wish is to be possessed by delight so you can be a Light to the world. You delight in a feeling of sacred unity.

Your personal agenda remains but it is not primary. Your personal purpose remains but it is secondary to Love's purpose. You are a Bright Field of radiant energy broadcasting that good vibration unique to you. You relax. It is not your concern how this gets done. Your focus is to ensure that you are in communion with the broadcaster and not obsessed with the collective broadcast of doubt and fear. This is the fear of the personal and collective mind that you identify with as the personal sense of, "Me, my and I." Possession is undone through detachment but this is detachment from thought and not from feelings.

DAY NO 7

ONE DAY

It happens on one day. It is always happening on one day. In this story of the Beautiful People the term "One Day" represents time. In today's world we are obsessed with time. We forget how to feel the Presence of the Timeless within each of us. In Irish mythology this Timeless place is called Tir Na Nog meaning the Land of the Forever Young. In Tir Na Nog one day is equal to many years. This only points toward reality. The Timeless is not an immeasurable amount of time. The Timeless cannot be compared to time because it is outside this mental concept. The logical and rational mind cannot grasp the experience of the Timeless.

Over time as you grow up you leave the unconditionality of gift receiving for possession by the personal mind. Metaphorically speaking you go to a far-off land. You become the lost Prodigal Son or Daughter who spends their birthright in the experience of separation from Source. You become your resourceful personal self. Then one day separation is who you feel yourself to be. You forget the One who is the Giftgiver. Your focus is on protection and acquisition rather than on allowing and giving from the emptiness that is forever full.

On this one day you have the choice between Love and fear. Each day your task is to remove the blocks to Love. The main block is your obsessive relationship to time and thought. You are under a collective spell that you learn to undo. This spell of separateness from Love will break on one day. It will be a glorious day. It will be a day of grace. For some time you will leave the boundary of time. In that Timeless moment you are The Ugly Duckling at the Lake of Revelation. Reflected back to you is the beauty of who you are. You are Snow White awakened from the sleep of the separate sense of self. You know yourself to be an eternal emanation of beauty expressing though the form of the body.

Each day your choice is to commit to realize Love's purpose as it created you to express through you. You give up the idea of the persona as your sense of the real you. You cultivate witness consciousness. This is the practice of observation and detachment. Do not confuse detachment with absence of feeling. Detachment is learning not to get sucked into the drama of the voice in your head. Detachment is learning how to be centred while the drama goes on round you.

One day will dawn and you feel the burden of time, thought and fear is not who you are. You leave the focus of the collective mind. You venture into the unknown so that you Return to Love. You leave The Matrix. You become a finder of the treasure that is the real you.

DAY NO 8

THE LEAVING

In The Hero's Journey the leaving is referred to as The Call to Adventure. This is the journey of learning to be true to who you are created to become. There is also the Refusal of the Call. Most of us opt for the refusal. We stay in the ordinary world. This is the everyday world of the known rather than venture into the extraordinary world of what it feels like to be known through. The Call to Adventure for each of us is to Return to Love. Life calls us to leave our sense of the personal self to go where no one has gone before. Others who have journeyed beyond that ordinary world of knowledge into Knowing can only point the way. They preach a sermon of union and sometimes they may use words. Mostly they preach through Presence.

There is a guidance system. It is your inner GPS. It is that Still Small Voice within. You usually don't hear it above the incessant noise in your head. It communicates through levels of heightened energy. Trust and feel its promptings and take action in response to such promptings. Patience and waiting are needed. You learn to wait without waiting. Strange as this might appear this is the most practical and beautiful way of living.

It may be unknown but it is new and creative. It is less stressful because you are not pushing the river. To share a Zen proverb, "The river flows and the grass grows by itself." To use a similar instruction from the Master Jesus, "Give no thought to tomorrow." (Matthew 6.34 KJV) You will protest, "Nothing will get done if I don't think about it. Science has measured ninety percent of the thoughts passing through the average person's mind as negative. Each thought produces a cocktail of chemicals that flow through the body. What chemical reactions do you think your personal mind is serving up to your body each day?

This everyday thinking is not thinking in a creative sense. It is unconscious static. You have not learned the power of being thought through. You have not learned faith in who you are as a co-creator with the Infinite. You have to leave the ordinary world of dualistic fear-based thinking and venture into unknowing. Metaphorically speaking you pass through The Cloud of Unknowing to access the Infinite Sky of Knowing. You leave Egypt to pass through the desert to get to the Promised Land. You give up belief for faith. You move from one who is a seeker to one who is a finder.

DAY NO 9

THE OCEAN

Those of the Tuatha de Danaan who still feel connected to Source energy leave The Ordinary World of fear and obsession now rampant in the four cities of the beautiful people. This is the ordinary world of the separate sense of self. This personal self can never fulfil you because it is time based. It ends. It is not your True Self. It does not allow you access to your soul or good vibration that is your feeling of communion with the Infinite.

The Tuatha de Danaan sail out on the Ocean toward another shore and a dimension yet unknown. To use a Biblical metaphor the chosen people leave the slavery of Egypt for the desert in search of the Promised Land. To use a movie metaphor, Dorothy leaves the gray world of Kansas to venture into the extraordinary world of Oz. Most of us want to play safe. We want the security of the known even if it means we feel we are dying inside. Often some form of crises arises that pushes us to go on a search to find meaning in what appears meaningless.

On this journey of life everyone travels their personal Road of Trials. A time comes when there is the breakthrough experience. You know this when it happens. You are no longer a seeker. You are a finder and a Knower. This breakthrough experience is a revelation that happens to you. You die to the personal sense of separateness and know unity. There is a time on this journey when there is much waiting. Patience is essential. The vastness of the Ocean is all around you. The quiet of the desert is all around you. There appears to be nothing happening. At least with the personal self you get to think and feel that there is always something happening.

Metaphorically speaking the ocean and desert will draw you into feeling more comfortable with silence. However, in the beginning you are likely to feel disturbed. You meet with the full force of the personal mind. You meet with the Madman in the Cave of the Skull who assures you that you are out of your mind. You will want to return to the ordinary insanity of obsessive over thinking. At least there is drama. Something is happening. You are required to stay on the ocean, in the desert if you want to know what it feels like to reach the other shore or reach the Land of Promise. On that other shore you learn to feel happy for no reason. You pour your life away from the fullness of the One Life. This is the meaning of the wisdom teaching of the Master Jesus when he says, "He who seeks, let him not cease seeking until he finds; and when he finds he will be troubled, and when he is troubled he will be amazed, and he will reign over the All." (Gospel of St. Thomas -Saying No 2)

DAY NO 10

FOUR TREASURES

Those of the Beautiful People who have not forgotten who they are and their connection to the Giftgiver leave the four cities. These are the cities of Falias, Gorias, Murias and Finias. However, they do not leave empty-handed. They leave the ordinary world of fear and possession with Four Treasures. One treasure comes from each city. From Falias they bring the Lia Fail - The Stone of Destiny. From Gorias they bring the sword which belonged to Nuada. From Finias they bring The Spear of Lugh. from Murias was bring The Cauldron of Plenty.

Unfolding The Story

In the story of *The Four Treasures of the Tuatha De Danaan*, these treasures, like the Beautiful People go underground. This going underground is symbolic of our energy and what we do with the gifts we refuse to share with the world. The reason this happens is for reasons of protection. We learn in different ways that we are conditionally acceptable dependent on our actions. We bury inside ourselves what family, culture and those in authority over us disapprove of. In this way we armour the body and stop listening to our inner guidance.

Creation created you to uniquely express through you. Allowing this flow of unique expression is to discover buried treasure. You are that treasure. To uncover and unearth this treasure is to know you are beautiful beyond measure. You are a unique expression of Infinite Love. You are gifted the form of the material body to express this Infinite Love through.

You are the treasure you seek in so many myriad ways. Many seek to fill the emptiness by gaining treasure on earth and miss the real treasure they are. From this treasure you pour away good vibrations that heal yourself and your world. The first step in reclaiming the treasure is to agree to the possibility that this potential is within you. You practice opening to this potential and not just believe in the possibility. This is not another system of belief. Through practice you claim your experiential Knowing. This is the practice of faith rather than accent to a fixed belief.

You have been given the gift of a human life. Modern science estimates the chances of getting here as ten billion to one. You are already one of the chosen. You have nothing to prove. You have the glorious opportunity no other creature on this planet has. You have the potential of knowing you and Creation as one eternal dance. In discovering the treasures within, you become a channel for the outpouring from an emptiness that is forever full. Follow the Call to Adventure to be the magnificence you are gifted to become. In this way you become one who is blessed and your fulfilment will be in blessing others from this sense of fulfilment.

Being Beautiful

DAY NO 11

THE HOLY LAND

The Beautiful People who still remember their connection to Source eventually come to a land later named Eire - Ireland. The poet and bard Amergin Glúingel names this land. He names this land after one of the three queens of the Tuatha Dé Danann, Banba, Ériu and Fódla. The poem *The Song of Amergin* is the first poem of this land of Ireland.

> *I AM the wind which breathes upon the sea,*
> *I am the wave of the ocean,*
> *I am the murmur of the billows,*
> *I am the ox of the seven combats,*
> *I am the vulture upon the rocks,*
> *I am a beam of the sun,*
> *I am the fairest of plants*
> *I am a wild boar in valour,*
> *I am a salmon in the water,*
> *I am a lake in the plain,*
> *I am a word of science,*
> *I am the point of the lance in battle,*
> *I am the God who creates in the head the fire*
> *Who is it who throws light into the meeting on the mountain?*
> *Who announces the ages of the moon?*
> *Who teaches the place where couches the sun?*

Here is celebrating the connection to Source where the personal "I am" is unified with the One 'I AM.' In the words of the Master Jesus "I and my Father are one." (John 10:30 KJV).

Unfolding The Story

This is an Irish story but it is not only relevant to anyone who lives in Ireland or has Irish ancestry. The land of Ireland is symbolically the land of wholeness. W. B. Yeats invites this experience of wholeness in his poem I am of Ireland

> *I am of Ireland,*
> *And the Holy Land of Ireland,*
> *And time runs on,' cried she.*
> *'Come out of charity,*
> *Come dance with me in Ireland.'*

W. B. Yeats

This is an invitation to embody wholeness and that which is holy within you. Whole and holy are etymologically speaking words that stem from the same root meaning. The Holy Land, The Promised Land is not a physical place. It is a state of being existing within you and expressing through you. Your work is to invite its revelation by getting out-of-the-way. You are standing in your own light. You are here to know yourself as one of The Shining One's. You are this glorious. As the poet William Wordsworth declared in *Intimations of Immortality* from *Recollections of Early Childhood*

> *Our birth is but a sleep and a forgetting:*
> *The Soul that rises with us, our life's Star,*
> *Hath had elsewhere its setting,*
> *And cometh from afar:*
> *Not in entire forgetfulness,*
> *And not in utter nakedness,*
> *But trailing clouds of glory do we come*
> *From God, who is our home:*

William Wordsworth (1770-1850)

This experience of glory is your birthright. Your birth arises from the rightness and goodness of non-separateness from Love. This is what it is to be born again. You are, metaphorically speaking, born again to the extent you live as the Presence of Love in form. You allow your personality to light up from within. You become a Light to the world but you know this Light of Love is not yours. It is not a possession. It is who you are as an emanation of the One Light, the One Life and the One Love.

Being born again is not the result of some weekend high at a retreat or Mission. It is not a cerebral accent to some belief. If it were only this then the world would be a different place. There would be Heaven on Earth. It is much more challenging than an affirmation of belief. You have to be willing to claim your own authority and take the adventure into the unknown. You have to be willing to leave the security of belief and, metaphorically speaking, venture into the desert to find the Holy Land that is your personal knowing of wholeness.

DAY NO 12

THE SEARCH BEGINS

The search will only begin if there is a longing to be more than you think you are. You cannot know the beauty you are unless, in the words of W. B. Yeats, you are willing to take the great adventure into learning how to "companion your greatness." You go on a quest. You confirm, and learn to trust, wisdom teaching through your own experience. Are you prepared to be a Knower or remain a believer or a non-believer? Will you be certain or live in doubt? Without the breakthrough of revelation there can only ever be a belief in your own magnificence. Wisdom teachers affirm this magnificence that is within you but they know it has no meaning unless it is your direct felt experience.

I was taught as a child by those who had no experience of revelation. They were the blind, not so much leading the blind, but the blind making others blind to their own beauty. It is still the case today. This is the meaning of the statement by the Master Jesus when he said, "But woe unto you, scribes and

Unfolding The Story

Pharisees, hypocrites! for ye shut up the kingdom of heaven against men: for ye neither go in yourselves, neither suffer ye them that are entering to go in." (Matthew 23:13 KJV)

The search begins in earnest when you commit to feeling and trusting in your Y.E.S. The acronym Y.E.S. stands for Your Energy System. Trusting your energy is illustrated in the Russian folktale *Vasilisa and the Magic Doll*. This doll comes awake whenever it needs to guide Vasilisa the Beautiful on her adventure to fetch light from the Baba Yaga. Baba Yaga is a figure from Slavic folklore. She is a dark goddess, fierce like Kali or Hecate, a wise, wild crone, a demanding figure who may set you off on a heroic task to test your mettle.

> *Journey from the self to the Self and find the mine of gold. Leave behind what is sour and bitter and move toward the sweet.*
>
> ~ Rumi

In many fairy tales the hero is feminine. Many of these heroines are named Beauty. There is Bella (meaning beauty) in *Beauty and the Beast*. There is Sleeping Beauty in the fairytale of the same name. There is Vasilisa the Beautiful in the Russian fairy tale of the archetypal wise woman Baba Yaga. Why all this feminine energy? It is because beauty is receptive, is allowing, is birthing. Force is not the dynamic. It is a falling in Love.

Many of us feel that in the grand scheme of things our contribution does not matter. Once you experience At-One-Ment you know your contribution matters for all-time. Your contribution to unity makes a difference. You are living at the leading edge of evolution which is the union of form with the Formless and the union of time with the Timeless. This is to go where no man or woman has gone before. Going on this journey of companioning the greatness inside is unique to you. You are a religion of one. There are seven billion revelations of Love available on this planet. If you awaken to the magnificence of your True Self your impact in the world of time and space and beyond is significant.

Being Beautiful

You are a force to be reckoned with. As the Mentor of the hero Luke Skywalker in the movie *Star Wars* (1977) Obi-Wan Kenobi teaches, "Feel the Force Luke." He does not teach the hero to think about the Force or believe in the Force. To access the power of the Force to light up the darkness requires you learn to <u>feel your connection</u> to this Source energy.

DAY NO 13

THE STONE OF DESTINY

You are here to embody the magnificence of Love in form in a unique way. This allows the Light of Love to radiate through you. This experience of radiance lights up the personality and you delight in who you are. You are in joy of your true Self. In my experience far to many seekers try to transcend the form of the body. There is only one effective way to transcend anything. You transcend through loving what you are trying to transcend. You love it so much that there is no longer any sense of separateness. Some religious groups teach avoidance of the world. There are certain religious teachings that state that matter is evil. Such teachings clearly show they are created from ideas of the personal mind rather than from direct revelation from Source.

The first treasure of the of the Tuatha de Danaan is The Stone of Destiny. The Stone of Destiny screams when the rightful King of Ireland sits on it. In this story the rightful King of Ireland is you. The Stone of Destiny is the form you are. The Voice in the Stone represents the Still Small Voice within. The voice in the stone has to scream because you are not listening. It screams by way of crises. You become seriously ill. You end up separating. You lose your job or your career. You experience some form of suffering. This is not a punishment. It can be a Call to Adventure to create meaning. You go on the quest to reveal your Kingship. Kingship is not gender specific. It is representative of your sovereign nature. You return to the Palace of Presence and reclaim your sovereignty from the servant who has taken over your Kingdom and is running amok. This servant is your personal mind that thinks it rules the show. It will consign you to your fate rather than lead you to manifest your destiny.

> *Go placidly amid the noise and the haste and remember what peace there is in silence.*
>
> ~ Max Ehrmann

You will have found the first treasure when you commit to sitting in silence and listening to the silence within you that speaks through you. You trust this to express through you. You listen and attend. Out of this attendance you will be given to act. This is not immediate. You relax into trusting the moment. This is the practice of faith. You have faith in the unknowing and all knowing silence. Silence is not divisible. As the German mystic Meister Eckhart says, "The nearest thing to God is silence." He might have been more accurate had he said, "The nearest NO-THING to God is silence. The treasures of the Tuatha de Danaan are not things. They are living qualities you feel into and use. You use them or you lose them.

DAY NO 14

THE SWORD OF NUADA

The second treasure of the Beautiful People is the Sword of Nuada. The sword represents the way in which you use the power of intention. Everything manifested within this world of time and space is created from the Infinite Field of Intention. You are a co-creator with this infinite field. The choice you have in each moment is to follow the call of The Voice in the Stone that leads you to fulfil the destiny you are created to express in this world.

Being Beautiful

The sword is like the symbol of a cross. It has a vertical aspect represented by the blade. It has a horizontal aspect represented by the hand guard. The vertical represents the experience of the Timeless. The horizontal represents time. The sword is the unity of the two. The sword can be used in the service of the King you are or in service to the sense of separateness that you think you are. The choice is yours. This is the meaning of the Biblical statement, "No man can serve two masters: for either he will hate the one and love the other; or else he will hold to the one and despise the other. Ye cannot serve God and mammon." (Matthew 6:24 KJV) The sword of intention is two edged. You choose either the direction of unity or the direction of deeper separation. Unity is your destiny. Separateness can be your fate.

> *To realize one's destiny is a person's only real obligation and when you want something, all the universe conspires in helping you to achieve it."*
>
> ~ Paulo Coelho, The Alchemist

You claim the second treasure each day when you consciously use your intention in the service of the inner King/Queen. This represents the way in which Love's purpose expresses through the form of the body. The sword is a weapon of discernment. It is a weapon of duality. When used rightly the sword guards the doorway of the Higher Mind. You do not use the sword to destroy. It is used to protect.

The Sword of Nuada is claimed by one who would be the witness. Their intention is to allow The Voice in the Stone to speak rather than scream. The witness guards the doorway to the Palace of Presence from the Madman in the Cave of the Skull who would have the King/Queen confined to the dungeon. The holder of the Sword of Nuada witnesses the drama caused by over-thinking of the personal mind. They do not fight this over-thinking. They simply witness the drama it causes.

DAY NO 15

THE SPEAR OF LUGH

The third treasure of the Tuatha De Danaan, the Beautiful People, is The Spear of Lugh. This treasure represents your ability to use the power of focus. What you focus on expands. Those who would claim this third treasure are intent on moving from the personal Will to Power to the allowing of the Will to Love. Your focus is on alignment with Love's Purpose. This is your primary intent. You stay centered. You are not pulled this way and that. You do not allow yourself to be distracted by distraction. You have as the central focus of your life the opening to the emptiness that is forever full represented by The Cauldron of Plenty.

> *When you are able to state what you are for rather than what you are against, you are focusing on the potential for positive change. Once that is in place, you will find whatever you are focusing on expanding.*
>
> *- Wayne Dyer*

The Spear of Lugh is symbolic of one-pointedness. One-pointedness is the ability to concentrate. This is a key skill in learning how to direct your attention in the service of Love's purpose. Concentration is relaxed alertness. The Spear represents your ability to bring your awareness to whatever is in front of you. It is key to developing witness consciousness. This takes you beyond opposites and beyond the war going on inside your head. The ability to focus your energy is key in learning to enjoy your life.

The shaft of the Spear of Lugh represents the vertical dimension of time and space. It represents the Timeless or the Forever Now. It symbolizes the ability to be present to the moment. You can move beyond the horizontal dimension represented by thought. Thought takes you into time. It takes you to the past or the future. Your role as holder of the Spear of Lugh is to live the remembrance of NOW. This is the only time there ever is. The head of the Spear of Lugh is like a diamond. It represents laser like focus. This is the kind of focus you need to keep your personal mind from being taken over by the Madman in the Cave of the Skull. This is the personal mind that keeps you trapped in the prison of separateness from the REAL you. Without focus you miss much of your life.

> *Only one thing has to change for us to know happiness in our lives: where we focus our attention.*
> - Greg Anderson

Focus is relaxed focus. It is used in the service of Intention. Intention is direction without a goal attached to it. It is not goal setting which is direction with a goal attached to it. A goal comes with an attachment to a result. As a result it comes with inherent stress if you do not attain the goal in the way you wished. Intention is more general. For example, your intention may be stated as, "Thy will be done." This is not goal focused. You open to Source and allow your energy flow to guide your destiny. You steer your intention in the way you want your life direction to go rather than be driven by habit and reactivity caused by ingrained thought patterns.

Focus is learning to place your attention in service of intention. You focus on what you want rather than what you do not want. You do not fight what you do not want. You witness it. You use the power of focused awareness to direct your energy so that Source energy can express through you. This is not practicing affirmations in an attempt to create different results. Affirmations are simply more thinking usually layered on top of more powerful thoughts that are energetically in opposition to what is being affirmed. You use the power of focus to relax the body, practice refined breathing and stilling the mind. Focus is intention without the tension. You relax into opening to a higher power that directs you to realize the magnificence it created you to be.

Unfolding The Story

DAY NO 16

CAULDRON OF PLENTY

The fourth treasure of the Beautiful People is the Cauldron of Plenty of the Good God Dadga. This is symbolic of the human heart and mind in alignment with Universal Mind of which you are apart but never apart from. The Cauldron of Plenty is both empty and full at the same time. This represents your openness to channel the Message of Love. This is not your personal message. It is how the message of Love is allowed to flow through you.

You practice self-emptying so you can fulfil Love's purpose. This is your joy. You pour forth the blessings that are poured your way from the One who is the eternal Giftgiver. Your cup overfloweth with goodness and mercy. This is a goodness beyond moralistic judgment. This is not simply doing good but Being Good. You do not have to work out what is needed. You work at getting out of the way.

This is a different focus from that taught by The Law of Attraction where the focus tends to be on manipulating the Cosmos for your own ends. The Cauldron of Plenty is the truly attractive experience. It is beauty pouring from the Unmanifest into the world as Love in action. It feels natural. You do not drive this Law of Attraction through willpower. You draw it to you from the Field of Infinity. You willingly receive what Creation intends to give through you.

You willingly align with the dance of Love. In this way, in the words of W. B. Yeats you, "Come dance with me in Ireland, the Holy Land of Ireland." You feel whole. You feel holy but this holiness is not a script you live from but an experience you allow to live through you and as you. This flow moves through the body. You embody this plenitude that flows through you. It is not moving from your personal agenda. You give no thought unless you need to facilitate Love in action. You are intentionally attentive to the way you follow your inner guidance.

Being Beautiful

This is the invitation from the first commandment. This works when you learn to feel in Love with who you are created to express. You go out of your personal over-thinking mind and enter the silence that is the nearest NO-THING to God. You begin to know the Love you are. This journey of Love begins with encouragement and moves through different levels of vibration until you live as Essence. The less there is of you as the personal "I, me and mine," the more there is of the Infinite. There is no loss here. There is you feeling in tune with the Infinite.

> *The Universe knows what it's doing. So don't develop a big ego, and don't be afraid.*
> ~ Benjamin Hoff

You know that to lose your life as the personal sense of self is to gain the Knowing of you as an expression of eternity. You still live in time but you are the Timeless having the real time of your life. You are pouring forth the fullness of who you are from the willingness of an empty mind and open heart available to Love's Message.

DAY 17

THE FIR BOLG

The Beautiful People arrive on the Holy Land of Ireland. This symbolises the Call to Adventure into knowing the wholeness of who you are. The first people they meet are the people called the Fir Bolg. The name Fir Bolg translates as, "The People of the Baggage." These people represent you as one identified with the baggage of the personal self with your over-thinking mind and the burden of the past and anxiety for the future.

Unfolding The Story

In this story of *The Four Treasures of the Tuatha de Danaan* we are told about the Battle of Moytura where at the end of the battle the Beautiful People are driven underground. This is symbolic of the way we live our lives. The Battle of Moytura is always going on. When you identify with the drama of your personal life you are driving the beauty within you underground. You will not defeat the baggage through conflict. Fighting the baggage is the way you energize it further. You witness the drama rather than judge it. Over time the light begins to dawn. You are more than the story you think you are.

You are a Bright Field of Infinite awareness. This is the REAL you beyond the limits of "My story," with all its associated baggage. The choice is to stop doing battle with yourself. Choose to be in alignment with what cannot be divided. You cannot divide silence. You cannot divide no thought. What cannot be divided is the True Self. The Field exists. This field is the REAL you. It is where you are here to dance. You are not here to defeat the Fir Bolg. In this field that is beyond ideas of right doing and wrong doing there are no winners or losers. There isn't even the idea of the other. The Fir Bolg, the People of the Baggage, are with you every day. They are the people who irritate you, cut you up in traffic, take offence, ignore you or in some way push your buttons. They are reminding you of your own baggage. They invite the reactionary in you to do battle.

The most intense battle is inside your head. It is when you attach a feeling to a thought that floods the body with chemicals of emotion that in your own way you become addicted to. We become chemical reactionaries. Some of us live as incendiary devices awaiting ignition. Learning to be beautiful is learning to create the gap between reactivity and responsibility. There is a degree of consciousness operating. With practice you choose either to react from the baggage of the past or anxiety for the future or respond to the present moment as appropriate. Consciousness allows Beauty to resurface from underground where it is normally consigned. Allowing this arising is a win/win for all.

DAY 18

BURNING YOUR BOATS

When the Beautiful People arrive on the shores of the Holy Land of Ireland they burn their boats of silver and gold. There is no going back to what once was. They are committed. This is the beginning of a journey of faith. It is the willingness to venture into the unknown. You leave behind the known for the possibility of being known through. You will be in a battle for your REAL life but as the journey progresses you realize the way to win the battle is through letting go and through surrender.

Follow your bliss and the universe will open doors for you where there were only walls. - Joseph Campbell

You do not fight the Madman in the Cave of the Skull. You starve him or her of energy. You choose to go higher. You choose to be the witness without judgment. You become the witness of your thoughts rather than the one driven every which way by their arising that pulls you into emotional reactivity. You become still and know that you are so much more than your thoughts and emotions. You are the Presence that witnesses the drama. You are also the Presence that is the flow of the REAL you would that you move beyond right doing and wrong doing. You move beyond dualistic thinking.

Burning your boats of silver and gold represents giving up of beliefs not confirmed by direct experience. You become your own authority. The guidance you follow is from The Voice in the Stone. We follow other people's directions and the advice of experts. We have lost faith in our own capacity to know. We are not captains of our own ship. Follow the Voice in the Stone that leads to the fullness you are intended for. To listen to your inner guidance takes courage. You will feel alone. You will feel lost. You will not wish to burn your boats but keep them on the shore of time. In this way you hesitate and your heart knows you are doing so. You are not fully committed to companioning your greatness. You have doubts. We all have doubts. The choice is to have faith in that which is beyond doubt.

Your personal mind is where doubt arises. Burning boats of silver and gold is giving up attachment. You are moving to a new shore. This is the shore of the Timeless. This is the land where you realize your birthright. You unify opposition. You bring Heaven to Earth. You become a walking radiance in form. This is not as someone who believes and lives life from a given script but as someone animated from an eternal living Presence. This is your greatest gift.

DAY 19

THE ARISING OF BEAUTY

At the end of the day you will not remember the person with the most beautiful face but you will remember the person with the most beautiful heart and soul.

Unknown Author - At the End of the Day

In our Western culture we bury the beauty of Presence. Our children do not walk The Beauty Way. Our children are trained in the normal obsession that is over-thinking. There is a focus on looking beautiful. There is nothing wrong with looking beautiful but it is more in alignment with Life and your life purpose to be an expression of beauty. This beauty is not dependent on how your culture defines what it is to look beautiful. This beauty is an art you learn to allow to flow through you. It is already who you essentially are. Why not be true to this. This is what the poet Derek Walcott means when he declares in his poem *Love after Love*, "You will meet again the one who has loved you all your life. This is the One worth connecting with.

Being Beautiful

As with any art there are three requirements. These are:-

Commitment.
Discipline and
Patience.

We are conditioned to think we can have it all in an instant. In a paradoxical sense this is true because you are already an expression of the All One. When you really know this, however, you do not want for anything other than to be an outpouring of the blessings being gifted through you. It really is a different way of living in the world.

You do not engage in trying to transcend the world. This can be a subtle form of narcissistic self-interest. Let your interest be focused in bringing Heaven to Earth for the joy of everyone. You are not here to fix the world but invite a revelation about the world. You invite the end of the world. The wise know that the end of the world is not brought about through destruction. The end of the world as we know it means ending time as being the primary dimension you live from.

Being Beautiful needs your commitment. It is a most practical way of living but you need to practice and not just think about it. Become a disciple of The Beauty Way. Make this invitation to Essence meaningful to you. If Being Beautiful is only of lukewarm interest you can guarantee the antics of the personal mind will constantly distract you. Be committed and make a real contribution to bringing peace on earth. This is a peace beyond understanding. It is beyond logic. You will not understand how you could be loved so much. We are used to being loved within certain conditions. Let Being and feeling beautiful become a core value that you intend to live from.

This is the invitation from stories such as *The Ugly Duckling*, *Sleeping Beauty* and *Beauty and the Beast*. Each of these stories is your story. You are asked to undo the spell of separateness that you feel yourself under. You, metaphorically speaking, kiss yourself awake. You marry the frog you think you are. Most education is on teaching you that you are not ever enough. You live from an never ending sense of wanting. This always wanting is culturally conditioned. There is a part of you that feels empty inside. Our Western education system did not introduce you to the magic of emptiness. This magical way of living is symbolised by The Cauldron of Plenty whereby emptiness is fullness and you feel yourself forever enough.

> *The purpose of a storyteller is not to tell you how to think, but to give you questions to think upon.*
>
> -Brandon Sanderson

To undo the spell of separation you will need infinite patience. This is a different journey. It is a journey into the unknown. You are going where no one has been before because it is a journey only you can take. It is a journey into Love. All Lovers of humanity point the way but you are the one who has to walk the path. As the poet Antonio Machado declares, "There is no path. The path is made by walking." The practices are the steps you take to create the path. The walking is not thinking about walking the path. The walking is feeling the path being walked through you. It is a strange path because it is going NOWHERE except to NOW HERE.

You are forever one of the Beautiful People. The question is whether you value this gift of life enough to awaken to the magnificence of who you are? Like the character Neil Anderson (Son of Man in the movie *The Matrix (1999)* you could be The One. You could be The One who contributes to awakening humanity from the sleep of separateness that keeps us locked in the Matrix of suffering and time.

This is the choice you have. You are here to be a unique expression of Love's Message. Your life purpose is Love's purpose. You are given to know and be the knowing of this. You are this magnificent. Choose to be an artist. You are made in the image of God. God is Love. You are here to be this beautiful revelation. This revelation is the greatest gift you can give to the world. You are always at one with the Giftgiver. In this way you fulfil your destiny. You become a channel for the pouring forth of blessings. This becomes your only agenda. This is to be and do the Will of Love. This is beautiful and you know it. Make this your goal and you will come to know what it is to live happily ever after.

DAY 20

HAPPILY EVER AFTER

We come to the final day of our unfolding of this story of the Beautiful People. This is your story. It is a story that has no beginning or end. It is the story inviting you to know the beauty of the Timeless within. This is the meaning of the phrase that ends most fairy tales declaring, "And they lived happily ever after."

The 'Ever After' is not the experience of a long time. Happiness is the experience of flowing as an expression of the Infinite. Ever after never began and thus never ends. Happily ever after is the living experience of union and communion. In fairy tales it is the union of the Prince and Princess. There is the experience of awakening. Snow White awakens. Sleeping Beauty awakens. Each awaken from the sleep of personal identification with the limitation of "I am" to know the sacred unity of the universal "I AM."

This awakening to the happily ever after experience is a breakthrough. It is initially given by way of grace. You cannot enter this holy state through a personal act of will. You have to become empty so you can experience true fulfilment. You become a nobody so you can then be a REAL somebody. You then understand the Biblical statement, "He who shall be last shall be first." Do not, however, practice putting yourself last. You put yourself last by dying into Love.

The happy ever after individual is not living a life in pursuit of happiness. They are living a life of communion with Source. Happiness is a by product of feeling in alignment with the will of Creation which is the Will to Love. Their intent is to feel this communion and to allow the Giftgiver to give gifts through them. This feeling connection to Source is what it means to "Pray always." This is not prayer as petition in words from a sense of separateness but prayer from a feeling of energetic fullness.

> *Judge nothing, you will be happy. Forgive everything, you will be happier. Love everything, you will be happiest.*
>
> ~ Sri Chinmoy

The happy ever after individual is not happy all the time. When your life experience is lived only within the dimension of time happy ever after is not available. Within time you live in a world of duality. Real happiness within time is the outpouring of Love. This supports the realization and healing the idea of separation from Source is somehow real. Happiness is found in being in the world but not of the world. You live in the world of time but you have your awareness in the dimension of the Timeless - the ever after. You live your REAL story as a unique expression of eternity within time.

In this way you are one of the Beautiful People. You have discovered the treasure. The treasure is you but not the you that you think you are. You are one of the Shining Ones. You shine the light of Love into the world of darkness. This is the idea that separation from the Source of Love is real. You live as the treasure that is the REAL you open to being fulfilled in service to Love's purpose.

CHAPTER 6

The Practices

Physical beauty and ugliness is not very important. The real thing is the inner. I can teach you how to be beautiful from within, and that is real beauty. Once it is there, your physical form won't matter much. Your eyes will start shining with joy; your face will have a gleam, a glory. The form will become immaterial. When something starts flowing from within you, some grace, then the outer form is just put aside

– Osho - A Pearl of Exceeding Beauty

Being beautiful is an art. It is an unending art. It is the most practical way of living in the world. It will fulfil you in ways unknown to you. You are invited to experience real education. You are invited to the real university. This is the way in which the universe versus unity through you. This is not the way of logic. It is the way of unknowing. To have the universe speak through you is a journey of trust. You trust the Universe has your back which it does.

Much of learning to be beautiful is really a process of unlearning. You do not learn how to be beautiful. You learn how not to get in the way of the beauty that wishes to reveal itself through you. Being beautiful is practical for everyday living. To facilitate this practical way of living I share with you twelve practices. There are three practices related to each of the four treasures of the Tuatha de Danaan. This is a progressive program of practice. The first three are foundational practices but all the practices are important in their own way.

The Practices

This is the universe-ity education you never had. It is where you learn how to allow the universe to sing through you. The universe doesn't sing just any song through you. It sings a unique song through you would that you allow it to be done. Begin to verse yourself in the way of beauty by learning practices that turn you into a work of art. In the process you allow the beauty you are to be the work you do. This is the work of Love.

PRACTICE NO 1

BREATHING

Listening moves us closer, it helps us become more whole, more healthy, more holy. Not listening creates fragmentation, and fragmentation is the root of all suffering.

~ Margaret J. Wheatley

The Stone of Destiny is the body. The Voice in the Stone is that Still Small Voice within which in the story screams when the rightful King/Queen of the Holy land of Ireland sits on it. The Still Small Voice doesn't actually scream. To do so would violate your right to choose. It is more that the voice shouts through the experience of the body being flooded by delight because of awakening to knowing your Kingship or Queenship.

It is through the body that the revelation of Kingship/Queenship is declared. It is through the body that the resonance of Love's Message is known. You, as the rightful King/Queen of the Holy Land of Ireland are here to embody the Presence of Love. This is the Battle of Moytura. This battle is always happening. It is the battle for the command of your mind. Mind and body are not separate. What impacts one impacts the other. It is essential you have command of your personal mind. This is not a practice of mind control.

Being Beautiful

Neither is it a practice of programming. It is a practice of getting out of the way.

It may appear strange at first but to walk The Way of Beauty requires you to learn how to breathe. This is a foundational practice. More than any other practice this one practice is essential. It is essential because it is the key to learning to take command of the personal mind. Most everyone does not breathe in a conscious way. Most bodies are armored to some degree to prevent feelings that the individual does not wish to feel. The way we tend to control emotions we do not wish to experience is through some form of unconscious breath control.

Most people in the West are chest breathers and not belly breathers. This is especially the case with women who are culturally conditioned to pull their stomach in. In this way they restrict the free flow of their energy. This is happening more to young men intent on developing the culturally required six-pack. Psychoanalyst Sigmund Freud when asked, "What was the one thing you should do to preserve ideal health relied, "Keep a soft belly." It is not simply symbolic that statutes of the Buddha represent him as big bellied.

When was the last time you went to a doctor and they inquired of you as regards the way in which you breathe? There are many reasons conscious belly breathing is essentially the first step in learning to walk the Beauty Way. The first reason is because through conscious breathing you reclaim command of the personal mind. You take command of your life force from the Madman in the Cave of the Skull. If this is not done then your everyday life will be the battleground between you and the People of the Baggage. The People of the Baggage are your unconscious thoughts.

Most people walk this world of time and space burdened by two heavy suitcases. One piece of heavy baggage we call the past. For many there are labels attached to this suitcase that lead to depression. The other large piece of baggage is anxiety for the future. Learning to breathe in a conscious way allows you to put this heavy baggage down and relax.

The Practices

Most of us are over-thinking programs of reaction. This is the normal insanity of the modern mind. You have no real peace of mind and your personal mind will never allow that to happen. Thoughts arise and you are conditioned to react emotionally. Conscious breathing moves your centre of gravity from the Cave of the Skull to the belly. In Japan this centre is called the Hara. The modern mystic Karlfried Graf Dürckheim writes about this centre in his book *Hara: The Vital Center of Man*. (10) Conscious breathing takes you into awareness of finer feelings. When you use the common everyday expression, "I feel fine," you are referring to the fineness of the breath. The breath becomes so refined that you find real peace of mind. You feel so fine.

> *Emotion arises at the place where mind and body meet. It is the body's reaction to your mind - or you might say, a reflection of your mind in the body.*
>
> ~ Eckhart Tolle

Practicing conscious breathing is like taking steps in learning the art of karate. In the movie *The Karate Kid* (1984), the young hero Daniel LaRusso is mentored by the old man Kensuke Miyagi. His training consists of learning to wax the floor. The instruction is simply, "Wax on wax off." Conscious breathing is breathing in and breathing out. Like the Karate Kid you may well protest, "But I want to learn Karate." Or in your case, "But I want to feel beautiful." It is only later that you will recognize the value of this seemingly non-related practice.

The breath will be the way you return to being present. You reconnect to Source through feeling fine and feeling the refinement of the breath. You feel centered in the belly. Conscious breathing takes you come out of the Cave of the Skull. The King/Queen is present. The servant, that is your personal mind, is available to serve when sought to do so. This provides the foundation for walking The Beauty Way and following your destiny.

To find the treasure that is The Stone of Destiny you return to the body. You invite the experience of full embodiment. This is not a mental concept but a felt experience. What anchors you within embodiment is conscious breathing. How often in your journey through life have you been taught this foundational practice for learning how to feel fine and live a refined life? Conscious breathing is the first step in learning how to treasure the Life you are.

PRACTICE NO 2

LISTENING

The heart knows what it wants, and it often makes no sense. Intuition, creativity, and listening are all imperative in creating an inspired life.

~ *Jonathan H. Ellerby*

There are reasons The Voice in the Stone of Destiny screams. The first reason is you are not listening. The second reason is you do not feel worthy enough to be magnificent. You are conditioned to listen to every voice but your own. The Voice in the Stone is the voice that allows you to march to the sound of your own drummer.

If you think you are never enough then this will be your experience. This is not to invite you to become a positive thinker. Positive thinking is simply more antics of the Madman in the Cave of the Skull. You are invited to be a knower of the REAL you. The thought that you are never enough is the spell you are under. That spell is broken when a grace moment reveals who you are. You begin to step into having faith in the potential within. Through the practice of The Way of Ease we begin with encouragement. For most people moving from feeling like an Ugly Duckling to a creature of grace and beauty does not happen overnight although it can.

Learn to listen to the way in which The Voice in the Stone speaks to you and through you. Do not take this speaking through you literally. There is a voice that speaks through you but in the experience of this writer only rarely does this voice actually use words and usually only when you have crossed a threshold of consciousness. The Voice in the Stone speaks when you are in a natural state of heightened energy. You are happy for no reason. You Love for no reason.

Learning to listen is learning to feel attuned to your energy and the way in which the universe says Y.E.S. through you. Begin with the possibility of Y.E.S. rather than NO. First learn to listen to the voice inside your head that you take to be your ability to think. Listen to this badly tuned radio full of static. It is a never ending stream of tangential ideas. These ideas attach to a feeling. Before you know it you are in a mood or unhappy for a reason that has no relevance to the present moment.

> *To understand the immeasurable, the mind must be extraordinarily quiet, still.*
> — *Jiddu Krishnamurti*

Be assured this is a real challenge. The more you awaken to the overthinking mind the more aware you become of the insanity that goes on there. Your mind is in part a reflection of the collective insanity of the human mind reflecting the divisions within the world. Simply listen to this voice in the head. Do not fight it. Do not try to change it through positive thinking. Positive thinking is trying to change thoughts when it is the over-thinking mind that is the issue. You are being invited, not to change the content of your personal mind but to reach a clearer understanding of the structure of your personal mind and its relationship to Universal Mind.

Simply witness the thoughts without judgement. Allow them to come and go. Do not give these random thoughts energy. Begin to recognize that you are not the thinker but the one who is the awareness in which thoughts arise and fall. This practice of awareness watching awareness is a bit like practicing musical scales. It isn't sexy but it is necessary if you intend to learn how to treasure the REAL you. In this way you undermine the spell you are under.

Being Beautiful

This spell of over-thinking reduces your life to words, labels and beliefs. Words are useful but they are only fingers pointing at the moon. Get still and listen to your inner guidance that is The Voice in the Stone. Listen and learn to go beyond the personal mind that is always turned on but has you tuned out.

This practice of listening is an invitation to prayer. Prayer is not some form of cosmic ordering. It is opening to connection and communion. You listen without a personal agenda. You state your intent clearly. This intent is linked to your true heart's desire. You explore this true heart's desire as part of your alignment with destiny. Your true heart's desire is what brings you alive. It is felt when you are true to the one you are created to become. Prayer is where you invite yourself to meet again the one who has loved you all your life and knows you by heart.

PRACTICE NO 3

SITTING STILL

Not to be able to stop thinking is a dreadful affliction, but we don't realize this because almost everyone is suffering from it, so it is considered normal.

~ Eckhart Tolle

To realize your destiny listen to The Voice in the Stone that is the Message of Love uniquely wishing to express through you. Sit on The Stone of Destiny. This is a metaphor for some form of meditation practice. Without the practice of meditation, prayer or contemplation the voice in the head will rule your outer life. The King/Queen will not be heard.

Many people try meditation and declare it does not work. This is the whole point. It awakens you to what is not working. It awakens you to the fact that your mind is really not your own. This is not flattering to the personal sense of self. The personal mind tries to find some peace of mind when it is the very dynamic that blocks any real peace of mind.

Meditation comes in many different forms to suit different temperaments. Explore different techniques to find one that best suits you. This does not mean you have to sit in a formal meditation posture. The technique I use is Yoga Nidra. You do this practice while lying down. In the beginning this practice is supported by guided instruction.

Whatever form of meditation you choose to explore and practice be assured you will resist such practice. You will seek experiences of bliss and you find nothing happening. You are, metaphorically speaking spending time in the spiritual desert. It took Moses forty years of searching in the desert. You have the advantage of Beginners Mind. Remember you are cultivating an art. This requires patience.

You are cultivating faith in the unknown. You learn to stay in what is unknown. You are practicing allowing. You are practicing getting out of the way. You are trained to drive your life from the focus of personal power. Through the practice of meditation you learn to be drawn into the power of the Universal. This is real university education. It will set you alight but probably not in the beginning. You practice without expectation. Expectation will come when you are more adept at feeling centred.

> *The greatest revelation is stillness.*
> *~ Laozi*

Stay with whatever form of meditation you choose for a time. If you are unsure of what practice might suit you then you might like to explore a course of instruction available at www.awakeanddare.com. You are here to claim your birthright as King/Queen of your unique destiny. Only you can do this. Only you can allow this. No one can be more committed than you. The rewards are beyond measure but the challenges are equally as great.

Being Beautiful

In sitting still and doing nothing you go against most everything the present world culture says you need in order to be happy. You are not taught to breathe in a way that makes you feel fine. You are not taught how to listen nor are you taught the paradoxical power of the stillness that speaks.

Sitting on The Stone of Destiny is not a one-off event. It is a daily event. You consciously choose to remember your Kingship and Queenship. You remember your sovereign state. Let this practice of meditation be your contribution to changing the wasteland of separateness that is the personal mind into Heaven on Earth that is alignment with the One Mind. Let this practice be your contribution to mitigating the insanity of the personal mind that creates most all the suffering on this planet.

Your contribution counts. Your intention matters. What thoughts and emotions you broadcast into the ether matters for all time. The choice is yours. The Stone of Destiny is the first of the treasures of The Tuatha De Danaan. Your ability to claim them is progressive. The first requirement is to use each treasure as you find it. Begin by sitting and listening to the Still Small Voice within. In this way you take command of the Madman in the Cave of the Skull through conscious breathing. If this is the only treasure you claim then it will make a positive difference to how you live your life and the contribution you make to the human collective. However, there will be resistance. The Master Jesus says in the Gospel of Thomas, "First you will be troubled then you will be amazed." You will feel troubled to begin with because you will feel disturbed by how little command you have of your thoughts. Later you will feel amazed at how you can allow the Universe to think through you and create through you.

Claiming your destiny is not rocket science. You follow your destiny by tuning into your energy and listening and feeling how it is moving through the body. You are a feeling human being. You are here to feel and thus know yourself to be a unique expression of Love. This is the REAL you. This you will treasure. You learn to be still and know that your personal 'I am' is a unique flow of the one I AM. This is Kingship. This is Queenship. Will you listen to your sovereign self and crown yourself with the glory you are here to shine into the world? This is your destiny. Treasure it and honour it.

PRACTICE NO 4

NON-JUDGEMENT

As rain falls equally on the just and the unjust, do not burden your heart with judgments but rain your kindness equally on all.

~ Buddha

The Sword of Nuada is two-edged. It represents paradox. To invite the freeing experience of paradox you practice what appears illogical. You practice non-judgement. In this everyday world of duality you make choices all the time. This is until you learn to enter that state where you allow the universe to be the choice maker through you. You become so allowing that you live as a flow of the Divine.

In the story of *The Four Treasures of the Tuatha De Danaan* the sword guards the door of the Temple. The Temple is the Higher Mind. You claim the Sword of Nuada when you begin to cultivate the inner witness. The inner witness protects the sovereignty of the King/Queen in you. In practical ways you use the Sword of Nuada when you observe the antics of the personal mind. You use the sword when you witness the way in which you attach thoughts to feelings that become the drama of your life experience.

The Sword of Nuada is used to cut the energy of attachment to any thought you identify with that carries you deeper into feelings of separation from Source energy. Using the sword, your personal will, in this way you do no violence. You protect that dimension that would pour through you to bless you and the world. Through simply witnessing there is no build up of Karmic consequences.

In practicing silent witnessing there is discernment. You choose to be a witness rather than the drama. You do not judge your thoughts. That is engaging with the duality of the personal mind. It is more opposition. Neither judge yourself for ever judging yourself. This practice of non-judgement is the real practice called Jihad. It is the real Holy war going on in your mind. However, you cannot war with wholeness or that which is holy. The words whole and holy derive from the same etymological root.

Because you are under the spell of the personal self there is a war going on in your head. While paradoxically speaking you are always whole until you are less identified with the persona you will feel divided inside. Using the Sword of Nuada as an instrument of discernment takes you higher. It takes you beyond identification with thought and emotions into feeling connected with Source energy where you are then thought through.

Certain religious teaching refer to a future Judgement Day when everyone will get their just rewards. This will not be. Source energy does not judge and will never judge. Source energy is Love. The personal mind tends to be unhappy with the idea of non-judgement. It wants the bad guys punished. There are always consequences for unskilful action. This is the Law of Karma but this law is not vengeful. Within this Law of Karma there is available forgiveness and mercy.

As a skilled swordsman you learn to parry the energy that takes you into any reactionary behaviour. You protect your True self from your false self. You learn to treasure the REAL you. You use non-judgement and discernment to move into the energy field beyond right doing and wrongdoing. There you rest and recognize that division is created in your mind. Non-judgement is a practice of kindness. It begins with you. Source energy does not judge you. It never judges you. Non-judgement is the beginning of allowing. You allow your thoughts to flow. You allow your feelings to flow. In time you will have more experiences of being thought through. In time you will feel those higher and more refined feelings. You stop using your energy in repression. You are beginning to trust the REAL you.

PRACTICE NO 5

INTENTION

> *What I know for sure is that your life is a multipart series of all your experiences- and each experience is created by your thoughts, intentions, and actions to teach you what you need to know. Your life is a journey of learning to love yourself first and then extending that love to others in every encounter.*
>
> ~ Oprah Winfrey

The Sword of Nuada is a sword of clear intention. It represents the use of your personal will in service of your true heart's desire. It is the sword you use to protect Love's purpose as intended to express through you. The Sword of Nuada protects soul energy. Your personal mind will drive you to distraction. The Sword of Nuada protects you from being distracted from guidance of The Voice in the Stone. This voice allows you to know yourself as sacred unity. You are not here to develop the qualities of the soul but allow them to flow through you. All spiritual traditions hold the soul has every virtue.

Get still and listen. Set your intention to allow this guidance from the soul. Be still and know you are Love. The forces of separation will rise and seek to reclaim their position. Stillness allows Love's purpose to be your guide to their overthrow. The sword is, metaphorically speaking, the use of that energy for cutting what does not serve the clear intention of the soul. This writer defines the soul as your feeling connection to Source energy. It gifts you such virtues as beauty, truth, wisdom, abundance and Love. These are not qualities of the separate sense of self. They are not things you ever own. They are who you realize yourself to be. These virtues are given by the Giftgiver. They come through you to light up the personality. The holder of the Sword of Nuada is alert to the way in which the personal mind seeks to continue the spell it has the REAL you under.

The holder of the Sword of Nuada begins to be the guardian of refined feelings. They notice when the personal mind or the mind of another invites discouragement. We all experience this to some degree. Some people live their lives this way. In my own family there was little encouragement although there was not much discouragement either. The advice given us children was, "We only want you to be happy," With that general pointer we got on with life. In a strange way this is what has lead me to explore what it means to live "happily ever after."

> *Let yourself be silently drawn by the strange pull of what you really love. It will not lead you astray.*
> ~ Rumi

To support the REAL you there will come a time when you may need to change the company you keep. There are many well-meaning people who would have you play safe and stay within the boundary of the normal insanity of the over-thinking mind. They use a different sword to protect their sense of the personal self. The same invitation comes from the rather strange Biblical instruction, "If any man come to me, and hate not his father, and mother, and wife, and children, and brethren, and sisters, yea, and his own life also, he cannot be my disciple." (Luke 14:16 KJV) This is not an invitation to hatred but a recognition that the people most likely to hold you back from answering the Call to Adventure are those who are your family and tribe. Your self realization or self-actualization becomes a threat to the established order. If you live from fulfilment then no one can control you through suggesting you are not enough and need more things? You need nothing other than to share such fulfilment.

The Sword of Nuada is there to protect you from group dynamics that keep you locked into any group mind-set. There will be times, and even many times, when you grow beyond the consciousness of the group. There will often be a parting of the ways. Sometimes this is an amicable parting. At other times it is not. The one who claims the treasure that is the Sword of Nuada is loyal to The Voice in the Stone and not to any group dynamic that might insist that they adopt a specific belief. Listening to The Voice in the Stone can make you feel isolated. It is a real challenge to stay loyal to what is unknown but being birthed within you. This is why it is so helpful to have a Mentor or Soul Friend who has only one agenda. This is to keep you focused on being true to who you are created to be.

PRACTICE NO 6

PURPOSE

Everyone has a purpose in life...a unique gift or special talent to give to others. And when we blend this unique talent with service to others, we experience the ecstasy and exultation of our own spirit, which is the ultimate goal of all goals.

~ Deepak Chopra

The Sword of Nuada protects the heart's core value. However, American Priest and Theologian Matthew Fox declares in the Sounds True audio recording *Radical Prayer*, "In the end there is no protection for the heart." Still you are required answer the Call to Adventure that is the heart's longing for union with the Beloved. You are invited to give those invitations that assure you that you are never enough.

The true desire of the heart is to follow the purpose of Love as intended to express through you. This is your called Sankalpa - your heart's intent and direction. In mythology storytelling this desire takes you to The Boon Tree or The Wishing Tree. You, metaphorically speaking, like the Buddha sit under this tree and wait to receive the boons you are here to give the world.

Being Beautiful

You learn to use The Sword of Nuada to protect your ability to receive boons. Your focus is not on getting but on giving. This is not so much giving of things but giving NO-THINGS. You protect the Cauldron of Plenty which is forever empty and forever full. Creation designed you and destined you to be a channel for eternal gift giving. Therein lies your fulfilment. Yours is a paradoxical journey of descent into fullness of emptiness.

This descent into emptiness goes against everything you are taught to believe in. You are taught to believe in ascension. "Who," you might ask, "Would willingly descend into NO-THING-NESS?" The answer is, "Only those who would trust the possibility that is the magnificence of Love's Message. The Sword of Nuada is a sword of protection. It protects you from that which would keep you spellbound and asleep in the tower of the intellect and over-thinking mind.

To claim the Sword of Nuada you need to know what you are protecting. You learn through direct experience to feel what is worthy of protecting. What is worthy are your finer feelings that express as creativity, compassion and Love. Your actions in this regard will speak louder than words. In my homeland of Northern Ireland there are many people who value loyalty. They are loyal to a particular union. This is the union of Northern Ireland with the United Kingdom or loyal to the desire for a unified Ireland. The individual who would claim the second treasure of the Tuatha de Danaan is loyal to the real union. This is the union of opposites. It is the union of time with the Timeless. It is the union of the human with the Universal.

One love, one heart Let's get together and feel all right.
- Bob Marley, Bob Marley – Legend

A core value is not just central to the individual or tribe identity. It is allied to a principle of the Universe. What core value are you serving? What core value are you radiating into the world? Are you broadcasting thoughts and emotions of fear and mistrust? Are you clear about your life purpose? Without being clear, or at least willing to commit to such clarity, there is nothing to protect that is of real meaning. You are then on the journey referred to as *The Voyage and Return*. This is the journey of many people. It is the journey between birth and death where there is suffering but the individual finds no meaning within such suffering. There is no sitting beneath the Boon Tree. There is no ability to live as a radiance of well-wishing. You live your life between birth and death with the song you alone are here to sing never having been heard and shared in its fullness. This is the number one regret of people close to dying. Their wish is, "I wish I'd had the courage to live a life true to myself, not the life others expected of me."

What is worthy of protection are the feelings of encouragement, excitement and empowerment that allow you to radiate enthusiasm into the world. You become a broadcast of hope and well-wishing. You pour away those gifts received through you from the eternal Giftgiver. This is your delight. You sit silently beneath the Boon tree and willingly inviting the boon to be gifted through you. You are empty of a personal agenda except when needed to support your deeper purpose. You do not worry. You live the spiritual instruction, "Give no thought for tomorrow."

> *Home where my thought's escaping. Home where my music's playing, Home where my love lies waiting silently for me.*
>
> *- Simon and Garfunkel - Homeward Bound*

The Love light is not yours. It isn't something you own. It is who you are. It waits silently for you waiting to be voiced through you from the deep heart's core. You choose what it is you value and live it with all your heart and mind. This allows your heart and mind to be available to Source Energy. This is worth protecting because it invites you to become a channel for healing the primary cause of suffering within this world of time and space which is the personal identification with the sense of the separate self.

PRACTICE 7

FOCUS

One reason so few of us achieve what we truly want is that we never direct our focus; we never concentrate our power. Most people dabble their way through life, never deciding to master anything in particular.

~ Tony Robbins

The Spear of Lugh represents the capacity to focus. The energy used in repression and emotional reactivity becomes available for focus in service to the inner King/Queen. You use this focused energy in service to Love's Purpose. The spear is symbolic of one-pointedness. You make the personal will available to The Will to Love. This is the proper use of the personal will. One-pointedness is developed through practice. You focus on allowing the revelation of the treasure you are. This is more about letting go than about acquisition. You let go of over identification with the drama. You focus on developing witness consciousness. You live above the drama. This is the practice of detachment but not detachment from feelings. It is detachment from the energy process that takes you into the emotional experience of feeling separate.

Make your daily intention to point your energy toward Knowing and feeling your connection with the One Life. Focus is on removing all the blocks to Knowing you are Love. The practice of one-pointedness is not a focus on acquiring more information. It is a practice of present moment awareness. The focus begins with intention to be available to the present moment as it is and not how you would necessarily like it to be. This requires The Sword of Nuada. The personal mind will drag you into identification with the People of the Baggage. Their focus is on the past and the future which keeps them tied to the burden of time.

Focus and one-pointedness takes you into the body, the breath and the senses. You focus on living a sensational and inspired life. Your commitment is to embody Presence. You invite soul awareness. You are becoming your own Anamcara - soul friend. You are beginning to fall in love with the world. You begin to broadcast unity. The personal mind becomes available as the servant it is intended to be. Your focus is on being energetically available to Universal Mind. This is also your REAL mind.

> *We do not need to go out and find love; rather, we need to be still and let love discover us.*
> — John O'Donohue, Anam Cara: A Book of Celtic Wisdom

There comes a time when the experience and the experiencer are one. This is truly living the sensational life. You begin to know what love of Life really feels like. You know you could never earn this great blessing. You know that The Promised Land is as a living experience. It is not different from you. The difference is that there is no one to experience this Promised Land. Do not be frightened by the idea that there is no experiencer. You do not disappear. What disappears is the illusion of separation. You as the wave know that you are never apart from the Ocean.

Your life focus becomes learning how to feel centered. You begin this learning by feeling centered in the breath. The breath keeps you out of the distraction of the personal mind and in the body. The body keeps you in the present moment. You make it your intention is to stay above the drama of incessant thought that drives reactivity. This is the work you are required to do in each moment. This is the beginning of being unplugged from The Matrix. The Matrix is the collective program of separateness we are all identified with. Like the hero Mr. Anderson (meaning Son of Man) in the movie *The Matrix* (1999) we become "The One." We become at one with the One. Focus takes you into alignment with the One Mind.

Being Beautiful

The holder of the Spear of Lugh begins to know they are the treasure they seek and the channel through which that treasure is gifted. They become heart-centered. It is through the heart that you know the Message of Love. It is through the heart that you know the intimations of the soul. You are moving into the revelation that is The Cauldron of Plenty. This is where you open to receive all that Creation intends to give to the world through you.

> *I find hope in the darkest of days and focus in the brightest.*
> *I do not judge the universe.*
>
> ~ *Dalai Lama*

You surrender your personal agenda to allow the Universal agenda to be your fullest expression. You no longer do your life. You begin to let go into a healthy balance of doing and Being. You even let go of intentionality which is a focus of your personal will. You begin to live, "Thy will be done." Your life begins to flow from Love's Message through the open mind and heart that you have less need to protect from the collective pull of separateness and suffering. You are the movement of Love in action. You are becoming the REAL you. The treasure you are is known to you and through you. You feel blessed. Your focus is on sharing this blessing of being known through with the world for the highest good of all.

PRACTICE NO 8

FEELING

> *Feelings do not grow old along with the body. Feelings form part of a world I don't know, but it's a world where there's no time, so space, no frontiers.*
>
> ~ *Paulo Coelho, Brida*

The Practices

At the climax of the first Star Wars (1999) movie the hero Luke Skywalker is given a clear instruction by his Mentor Obi-Wan Kenobi. He is told, "Feel the Force Luke." Note the instruction to the hero is to, "Feel the Force." The instruction is not, "Believe in the Force, Luke." Belief and doubt are two sides of the same coin. To feel the Force you have to be one with it. It is never separate from you. It is not a concept. It is alive. It is the force of the One Life. This is the Force that destroys the Dark Star of separateness which is ultimately not real.

How often have you been instructed to feel the Force of Love rather than simply believe <u>about</u> it? In my personal experience there have been few such teachers. Without this ability to feel the Force we go over to the Dark Side. This is the darkness of the sense of the personal self. We identify with the personal mind and the persona (meaning the mask). We lose the knowing of our original face that is always beautiful. Being Beautiful is a felt experience. It is feeling from your natural state. When you present your original face to the world you are not thinking you are beautiful. Beauty becomes you. You walk The Beauty Way.

Those who would claim The Spear of Lugh focus on feeling The Force. Feeling is experienced through the body. It is living the sensational life beyond labels and concepts. Are you able to look at a flower or a sunset without labelling it? Try looking at something without labelling or describing it inside your head. The flower is not its name. If all you see is the name you are identifying the flower with a sound you make by clicking your tongue. You do not see directly. This is the degree to which the over-thinking mind has taken over your ability to be present to that which is beyond words.

Choose well. Your choice is brief, and yet endless.
~ Johann Wolfgang von Goethe

When I invite a focus on feeling I am not inviting emotionality. I am inviting letting go of emotionality for stillness that brings you alive. Many people only feel alive through the experience of emotionality. The more roller coaster their life experience the more they feel they exist. This is the life of the addict. We are all addicts to the over-thinking mind. To live as Beauty in form you need to feel your connection to Source as it flows through your body. Your first practice in learning to return to feeling is spending time feeling the breath as it enters the body. This invites fineness of breathing and is reflected in our everyday expression, "I feel fine." The focus on the breath takes you out of over-thinking into stillness. This does not happen overnight. It takes practice, discipline and commitment. These are the three essentials of learning any art and equally apply to the art of Being Beautiful.

The focus on feeling and sensing takes you out of labels and concepts into present moment living. This is mindfulness but it is not full of what you normally think of as mind stuff. If you stop thinking, if you stop labelling you think there is nothing. You feel empty. No thought. No emotion. At first it appears that way because you live the drama of thought and emotion with a focus on action. You do not enjoy the paradoxical power of stillness and silence beyond labels, thoughts and beliefs. You are not used to being a Nowhere man or woman that has the NO-THING of the Universe think through them.

> *Feelings come and go like clouds in a windy sky. Conscious breathing is my anchor.*
> *~ Thích Nhất Hạnh, Stepping into Freedom:*

Without labelling or thinking your senses become heightened. You begin to see beauty increasingly. You are using the Sword of Nuada to guard against the distraction of the over-thinking mind. You are more detached which is to say you are becoming more open. You no longer follow a personal agenda. Your focus is to be present to Love's Message and not to the constant never enough broadcasting from the Cave of the Skull. Nor from the insanity of the collective over-thinking mind. You begin to dance to the sound of your own drummer.

The Practices

One way I practice feeling present is when driving the car. There is no radio with constant chattering that is representative of the never ending talking in our heads. There is no advertising reminding me that I need something I didn't before think I lacked. My focus is on feeling myself driving the car through hearing, seeing, touching and to a lesser extent smelling. The challenge is to see how far I can drive without getting caught up in an internal conversation. This is a form of meditation practice you can do anytime you are engaged in driving. The anchor to the present moment is always to return to feeling the breath without trying to control it. Focus means choosing the breath over the over-thinking mind. Focus means choosing feeling over emotionality and drama. It means being a witness to the emotions and the drama. In this way you claim the treasure that is The Spear of Lugh.

PRACTICE NO 9

FAITH

> *Truths cannot be acquired from words out of other people's mouths. Before Truths can be internalized, they must come from one's own realizations and practices. Through a lifetime of personal practice, human beings are capable of revealing all of the secrets of the cosmic essence. You are your own best judge.*
>
> *- Buddha*

The final practice for the one who would claim the Spear of Lugh is the practice of faith. The way faith is practiced in many religions today is the opposite of what it really mains to be faithful. In the modern world the word faith has been turned into being certain that your way is the right way.

The first step on the road to true faith is to honestly admit whether you know who you are. It helps tremendously to have experienced what has been given such names as Satori or the Breakthrough Experience. This is where you are graced the direct knowing of who you are. The Universe embraces you and declares, "This is my beloved child in whom I delight." In the Breakthrough experience, which is always a great grace, you know the treasure you are. You have for one eternal moment stepped outside time. You have for one glorious moment known what it is to feel Boundless. You have for one beautiful moment known what it is to be Love's Message. There is absolute certainty. There is the complete absence of fear. You are the birthless/deathless One. All you want to do is pour this magnificence into the world. You don't stay there. The personal mind returns to grasp this magnificence. It becomes another experience that is 'my experience.' You cannot, however, grasp what you are. It is like trying to bite your own teeth.

What if you haven't had this direct experience of the REAL you? The chances are you will become a believer or non-believer until such time that you really want to be a Knower. To become a Knower requires that you move into that transition zone that is the experience of not knowing. This is the paradoxical experience of descent that is a falling upward. It is a descent into the emptiness that is forever full. If you are sure you have the belief, the words, the scripture without the grounding in the experience beyond words then you will be one who does not know. Johann Wolfgang von Goethe in his poem *The Holy Longing* says, "And so long as you haven't experienced this: to die and so to grow, you are only a troubled guest on the dark earth."

> *Knowing yourself is the beginning of all wisdom.*
> ~ Aristotle

The dying is always a dying to the idea of the separate sense of self. This is a focus on learning how to feel comfortable with not knowing and inviting the experience of being known through. In this way you open to claiming the treasure that is The Cauldron of Plenty which is forever empty and forever full. This paradox cannot be understood by the personal mind that operates in the world of duality. In the world of duality either something is full or empty or something in between. You cannot have fullness and emptiness at the same time. This is true at the level of the personal mind but not at the level of the Universal Mind. Don't believe what I am saying. Take the adventure into the unknown. Go into the silent nothingness that guides you home. There your thoughts escape you and your love light lives silently waiting for you.

Faith is a practice of letting go. It isn't a statement of belief. It is a personal choice you make about your relationship to the Unmanifest world. You do not have to be religious or belong to a group dynamic. You only need to desire to come home to the REAL you. However, it does mean having the courage to let go all the bad advice you have been given. You willingly descend from The Cave of the Skull into the heart centre. In between you give up any unwillingness not to know. You trust The Voice in the Stone to guide you. The guidance is by way of good vibrations arising from stillness and sensitivity to your energy flow.

> *Faith is an oasis in the heart which will never be reached by the caravan of thinking.*
>
> - Kahlil Gibran

Once you claim The Spear of Lugh through practicing focus, feeling and faith you open to receiving the final treasure of the Beautiful People. You are now at the threshold of the deep heart's core. You are committed to letting go and letting Love's Message be your message. You know the process. You have only to practice. This is practical focused, empowered living. It will take you into a sense of ease. This is feeling at ease with who you are. This does not mean you experience a life of ease where you get everything the culture declares is living the easy life. Your sense of ease is living life in alignment with Source. You take responsibility for using the treasures you have realized within. You no longer fully identify with the personal mind. You open to the grace of knowing the magnificence you are. You companion your greatness. This is not your personal greatness but the great feeling you experience living in alignment with Creation that creates through you.

You are now ready to cross the threshold where identification with the sense of the personal mind is secondary. Your primary identity is with the

Being Beautiful

REAL you. You are ready to be empty of your personal agenda so that you live the agenda of Love's Message. This does not mean you do not have a personal agenda. In all likelihood you will. However, Love's purpose becomes your primary life purpose. How you express this primary purpose is secondary. The Universe has your back. You know this experientially rather than something to believe in. You allow the Cosmic I AM to play through the personal "I am" that you were once so identified with and imprisoned by. You leave the Tower of the Intellect and come down to earth. The Sleeping Beauty in you is awake and ready to live happily ever after in union with the Beloved.

PRACTICE NO 10

EMPTINESS

You pray in your distress and in your need; would that you might also pray in the fullness of your joy and in your days of abundance.

~ Kahlil Gibran

Rather than focus on the word emptiness focus on the word receiving. The eternal Giftgiver designed you to receive gifts. What stops you receiving these gifts includes the idea that you are never enough. You might feel you need to be in control of what you receive because you are not sure if what you receive is what you personally wish for. You are not used to receiving gifts given unconditionally. This willingness to receive gifts arises from a knowing beyond the ability of your logical mind to understand. This happens for many people with the practice of prayer. They think their prayers remain unanswered but usually they remain unanswered in the way the personal mind wishes to have them answered. The prayer is more often prayed from a place of "I want," rather than "I am willing."

The individual who would claim the fourth treasure of the Tuatha de Danaan is allowing. They allow gifts that our poured their way to be received.

The Practices

Their focus is on feeling any blocks or resistance to the flow of creative energy moving through them. They take action to express this movement that is the Message of Love. This can be by way of dance, poetry, music, art, gardening, parenthood or coaching. You know what it is that you enjoy expressing. You are the one responsible for sharing that expressive energy with the world.

You have certain talents that you are here to give the world. Do this with a willing heart and open mind and you will be rewarded tenfold. However, do not make this another focus on giving to get. Pay attention to the level of excitement moving to enthusiasm from Essence. Commit to becoming a joyous receiver without conditionality. This opens you to the real experience that is The Law of Attraction. You are willing to have faith in the Infinite Field of Abundance that created you to express through you.

This allowing will bring up blocks that you place in the way of Love. Expect these blocks to come up. There will be resistance. We find it hard to receive something for nothing and give for no reason. We are all bargain hunters in the arena of Love. We have a sense of discomfort if we think the gift has not been earned. Many of us think we do not deserve the gifts freely given. However, you will come to know that the gifts you receive from the Giftgiver could never be earned. They are just to magnificent to be measured.

> *Every intention sets energy into motion. Whether you are conscious of it or not.*
>
> *- Gary Zukav*

You are told in the Bible that if you ask you will be given. (Matthew 7:7 KJV) The reality for most of us is that we do not completely trust this invitation. We have doubts. Having doubts is normal. Let it simply be feedback. Do not judge yourself because you doubt the unconditionality of the One Life loving you. For the most part this is not your everyday experience. It is an energy you learn to align yourself with through learning how not to do but to be. It is like a beautiful cloak you learn to wear. This is symbolized by the coat of many colours worn by Joseph. This coat of many colours is the radiance of the seven chakras when in alignment. The body is filled with Light and the light of Love.

Notice how this whole process of claiming The Four Treasures is, for the most part, a journey of letting go and allowing. It is not a focus on achievement. It is not a process of ascent which is the way the personal mind focuses on "My success." It is the way of descent into the emptiness of NO-THING out of which everything is unconditionally given. There is a real paradox to be known here. When you willingly become a nobody special you enter that state where the Universe can express through you. You are both empty and full at the same time. However, do not make becoming a nobody special a focus of achievement.

The heart understands the way of descent into the emptiness that is forever full. The heart becomes empty so that it can be filled by the Beloved. Learning to be empty begins with intention. Each day intend to trust the way the Universe wishes to flow through you. Mostly witness your inability to be true to this intention. Do not judge yourself badly. Simply observe. Just start again. As Rumi wisely advises, "Come, come, whoever you are. Wanderer, worshiper, lover of leaving. It doesn't matter. Ours is not a caravan of despair. Come, even if you have broken your vows a thousand times. Come, yet again, come, come."

You will break your vow, you will break your intention more often than you would wish. This is not failure unless you judge it to be such. There is no success or failure here. There is only practice. With trust and faith in allowing you invite the descent of higher feelings. It is your faith in this allowing that will make you whole. This is faith, not as a script, but as a feeling of trust in the Universe. It is a knowing that what is asked for will be giv en. You become one who experiences expectation. What allows this experience is emptiness. This is not the emptiness of despair. It is the emptiness awaiting expression from the fullness of Creation. Notice that the less there is of "I am, me, myself," the more there is available to the one 'I AM.' This is the experience of living as the REAL you and sharing the treasure you always are.

PRACTICE NO 11

FULFILMENT

Your most precious, valued possessions and your greatest powers are invisible and intangible. No one can take them. You, and you alone, can give them. You will receive abundance for your giving.

- W. Clement Stone

You are beginning to live a magical paradox. You are empty of the personal mind which you have willingly allowed to be still. You have gone to a real university. This is where you allow the Universe to express through you and as you. You are a page that is blank so the Message of Love can be written through you. You have not picked up more information. You have experienced what it feels like to be informed by Love's purpose.

There is less anxiety. You are not faced with myriad choices. According to recent research many young people are feeling more desperate. The reason is paradoxical. It is because they have too much choice. Anxiety comes because they fear making the wrong choice. When you make it your intention to be true to yourself then this is central to all other choices. You do not have to feel anxious about getting it wrong when you allow the fullness of the Universe to express through you. Neither are you concerned about the latest fear. This is F.O.M.O. It is fear of missing out. This is the obsession that many people, especially young people, have around having a mobile phone.

Being Beautiful

While connection to other people is essential to good health it is even more important for real health. The word health is related to the words 'whole' and 'holy.' After the age of thirty-five years it is essential that you begin the journey that is the Return to Love and the awakening of the Beauty that you are. Fullness is the experience of living from the flow of the Universe through you. Abundance is the natural state of the Universe and is your natural state. Living life from the obsessive broadcasting of the personal mind is not natural. It is a form of collective insanity. Our individual and collective focus is on the experience of scarcity. This mirrors our feelings of never being enough. It takes a great degree of intention to guard against this invasive belief of never being enough that then becomes the way we see the world.

You have only one real choice to make and to follow. This is to learn to be the receiver of the abundance Creation created you to be. Please note this receiving is not for your personal aggrandizement or to ensure that you get everything you want. Getting what you want leads to more wanting. This focus on wanting is a major block to receiving without conditions. The receiving is true when you feel what you receive lights you up from inside. You want everyone else to be given what you have received. There is no sense of lack. The Universe expands through you. The more you receive the more you will receive provided you do not take personal possession of what you are given. You receive gifts from the Giftgiver to share the gifts.

> *In our willingness to give that which we seek, we keep the abundance of the universe circulating in our lives.*
> ~ Deepak Chopra

Do not fall into the trap of becoming owned by the things you own and that then own you. Fullness is not a belief you adopt but a feeling energetic you live from. Commit to learning to let go into that state of emptiness that is forever full. This has to be experienced. This has to be your adventure into the unknown but not the unknowable. When you put aside your personal mind you create an emptiness which the Universe then pours into. To begin with it feels like nothing is happening. This new learning requires patience and non-grasping. Neither of these skills come naturally to us.

What you focus on expands. With The Cauldron of Plenty your focus is on opening to receiving through being empty. The challenge for many is not to dictate. Dictating to the Universe is what many people understand by The Law of Attraction. The Universe is not set up to give you everything your personal mind demands. The Universe does not experience you as separate from itself. The paradox to realize is the Universe gives you everything you want would that you get out of the way and allow it to do so. When it says, "Ask and you shall given" do not ask from the sense of the personal self. Learn to allow the REAL you. This will be your joy and fulfilment. From the overflow you will love pouring forth into the world the blessings you receive from the Giftgiver. Your intent is simply to be a humble channel for the magnificence of which you are graced to a part off but never apart from.

PRACTICE NO 12

GRATITUDE

Whatever we are waiting for - peace of mind, contentment, grace, the inner awareness of simple abundance - it will surely come to us, but only when we are ready to receive it with an open and grateful heart.

- Sarah Ban Breathnach

To live the treasure of being The Cauldron of Plenty requires the practice of gratitude. This practice cannot be recommended enough. It is a gentle practice. It takes you out of your head into feeling. As a beginner you may not feel grateful. This is normal. Gratitude is a feeling you may not be familiar with. The Western culture invites you to feel never enough. Through unending advertising you are encouraged to feel a constant dissatisfaction. You become a consumer rather than one who is a co-creator.

Any future sense of satisfaction comes from a focus on lack. There is nothing wrong in enjoying things but do not become identified with the thing enjoyed. You are so much more.

Gratitude is a progressive practice. Do it at least once each day. In time you begin to see the world more as it is than how you think it should be. You are present to Beauty. You begin to be surprised. This is because you are no longer seeing the world in a grasping way but in a responsive and open way. You no longer focus on getting what you want but on expressing thankfulness for who you are given to be.

There are any number of things you could be thankful for. Are you able to see? Can you hear? Do you have a roof over your head? Will you have enough food on your table today? Are you free to walk the streets? In your country do you have freedom of speech? Are you free to express your point of view? Have you shoes on your feet? Do you have clean drinking water? The list could go on.

Gratitude is a way to return to feeling rather than living your life as an over-thinking reactive personality tied to patterns of the past and living in fear of the future. Do not practice gratitude with an attitude that it might get you what you want. Practice with an attitude of exploration and adventure. Be open to what might happen. This practice will expand your energy and bring healing in ways your logical mind cannot comprehend. Be patient. To begin with not much appears to be happening. The effect is cumulative. If you do not feel grateful simply continue until you do. This is a bridge to coming more alive.

As an avid reader I have read many books by many wonderful teachers. Most every one of them recommends the practice of gratitude as a necessary step in moving beyond identification with the entrenched sense of the personal self. What you focus on expands. The culture has an interest in having you focus on what you do not have. It teaches you that you are never quite enough. The practice of gratitude goes against the focus of the collective. Gratitude raises your vibration and as a result it raises the vibration of the collective that is humanity. This changes the energy that you broadcast into the world. This good vibration that you broadcast is then available to be received by those tuned into the same wavelength.

Gratitude opens you up to recognizing fullness. You begin to let go into a deepening sense of wonder. Wonder is not something you own and nor do you need to own it. You do not have to earn it. You only need be willing to receive it. It is not a measure of success or failure. You do not have to belong to an in group to receive it. You only need to have a longing to express the One Life you are created to be. When you are graced a moment of awakening to the magnificence of who you are you will know that you could never be grateful enough.

> *Appreciation and gratitude are a must if you choose to become the architect of increased happiness and your own fulfillment.*
> *~ Doc Childre*

It is not enough to think about gratitude. You need to feel it. Not only do you have to feel it you have to extend it. It begins with intention, moves into attention and is fulfilled as Love in Action. In this way you practice tuning into a different wavelength. You tune into co-creating with Creation. You are tuning into the vibration of fulfilment. In time this is no longer a practice you do but becomes a way of living in the world. This is not positive thinking but feeling in alignment with the Force that thinks through you. You are guided to the treasure that fulfils your true heart's desire. You know that fulfilment lies in this direction. It isn't outside you. It comes through you. Your cup begins to run over and you pour blessings into the world. You cannot do otherwise. You pour into the world not to fix it but to celebrate it.

When you feel in alignment with the great fullness that is forever empty you know your joy is in being available. You are glad to be empty but not in a way that your life has no meaning. You recognize that true emptiness is a magical paradox. It leaves you with a sense of wonder. You are no longer so focused on doing your life. You allow life to dance you. You and the Lord of

Being Beautiful

the Dance are dance partners. The Force feels through you and delights in you. You become a light unto the world and this too is your delight.

CHAPTER 7

The Way of Beauty

The dawn has secrets to tell you do not go back to sleep.
- Rumi.

You are here to be a co-creator with Creation. Notice the word 'co-creator.' You are not here to dictate to Creation. Life is not designed to give you everything you want. It is designed to allow you to be everything you are uniquely created to gift the world. In gifting who you are you will receive more than you could ever want. You will be amazed. You will be filled with delight. For far too many people each new dawn has no secrets to tell. We act from the conditioned mind and not the magical mind. The dawn has secrets to tell you when you allow the magic of the miraculous mind to express through you. When Rumi says, "Do not go back to sleep," he is not referring to another ten minutes in bed. He is referring to the sleep of identification with the sense of yourself as separate from Source.

Learning to Be Beautiful is an art. It is not enough to read about what such art involves. I play music but there would be no music if I did not practice. To walk The Beauty Way needs you to move forward. This is your responsibility. Practice, discipline and commitment are required. You practice every day. Your commitment is to be in Love with who you are created to be. This is always growing but the culture, tribe and the collective unconscious will drive you back into feeling separate. This leaves you feeling not complete, lonely and isolated to some degree and often to a major degree.

Being Beautiful

THE MORNING

What is it like to walk The Beauty Way at least for one day? Such a day begins intentionality. You consciously greet the day and promise to honor it for the highest good of all. Rumi honors it when he says, "Thank you for the opportunity for another day of loving." This opportunity begins with you inviting such possibility to be experienced through you.

> *i thank You God for most this amazing*
> *day:for the leaping greenly spirits of trees*
> *and a blue true dream of sky;and for everything*
> *which is natural which is infinite which is yes*
>
> *e.e. cummings*

I give the first half hour of each day to practicing Yoga Nidra. This is a form of meditation involving a complete body scan. I feel the whole of the body step-by-step. In time this takes me into living more and more in an embodied way. I focus on feeling each part of the body from head to toe. I become aware of energy blocks at subtle levels. In time I move into feeling the Presence of beauty as a daily instance. This is a meditative state in which I feel thankful for Being. In Yoga Nidra I declare what I feel to be my true heart's desire. This is in essence to express the Will to Love, or as declared in the Lord's Prayer, "Thy will be done."

During this period of Yoga Nidra practice there is silence. There is awareness of the Madman in the Cave of the Skull who wants all the action. This drama is simply witnessed. Sometimes it does drive me to distraction. This happens. I do my best to be patient. Set aside time to tune into The Voice in the Stone (the energy of the body). Do not tune into listening to messages on your mobile phone. This is not focused attention but commitment to distraction. This is not intended to be a judgement. It is asking you to be clear as to what is of real value. This is the use of The Sword of Nuada.

Once I have practiced Yoga Nidra for one half hour and declared my Sankalpa – true heart's desire - I then enjoy a cup of tea. Following the practice of Yoga Nidra I write for around forty-five minutes or more. Again this is done in silence. When I finish writing I then listen to Kirtan (devotional music). I am practiced enough to allow the writing to flow. The blank page holds no fear for me. It is very much a love affair. It is the easiest way for me to feel connected to Source. On those days that I do not write I feel the day to be different. I feel less anchored and grounded.

It is not important that you adopt the practices that suit this writer. It is more important that you adopt practices you learn to love. Such practices, however, must include essentials such as clear intention, silence and witnessing. Begin any practice for ten minutes. If you say you do not have the time then you are affirming that you have no time for the Timeless within you. Your heart will know this. Your action or lack of action demonstrates your level of commitment. If you do not make the time you are signaling to your heart that the revelation of Being Beautiful is not for you. This is your journey. You are the one required to walk the path. Which path are you committed to walking? Will you answer the Call to Adventure or take The Voyage and Return journey without meaning that is the collective insanity of the over-thinking mind? Will you walk The Way of Beauty arising from the silence of The Voice in the Stone?

Your day will have a different structure from mine. However, there are only two real choices to be made. There is the choice to consciously embody Love's Message or not. The emphasis here is on the word 'embody.' You are created to express Heaven on Earth in a unique way. Most of us in our own way are expressing the hell of separateness. This is not entirely your fault but to change it is your responsibility. Let your focus during the day be to remain aware of the body - the whole body - so you learn to live as a body in full Presence.

Being Beautiful

Be alert to whether you are being driven by the mind or drawn from the heart. Anytime you are driving a car use this time to remain silent and become sensational. See how far you can drive without engaging in mind chatter. Witness how you might judge other drivers. Notice how you feel when you make such a judgement. Make the drive a meditation. Feel yourself sitting. Listen to the sound of the engine. Notice all the sounds. Notice if you mentally label everything that you give your attention too. This is all the normal insanity of over-thinking. With this practice driving is not a waste of time. It is not just getting you from point A to point B. It is a practice in awakening to a new way of being in the world. You use the car drive to be drawn into the deep heart's core.

During the morning ask yourself the question, "What am I broadcasting?" Are you lost in over-thinking or are you quietly centered in the fineness of the breath, alert, responsive, alive and mentally silence and empty. Remember, this is not an emptiness felt as any sense of lack. It is an emptiness open to receiving what is needed in the moment. There is no grasping. There is no thinking about the future unless there is a need. There is no getting lost in thoughts about the past unless there is a need. There is the intention to broadcast good vibrations from the field beyond good and beyond bad.

This allows you to be more creative. You are available to the fullness of Creation. You relax because who you really are is trustworthy. You begin to know the REAL you beyond the drama of over-thinking and emotionality. You begin to trust that life will organize the essentials. You ask and receive provided you complete the cycle by receiving unconditionally. You are more intentional in asking. You align your intention with your Sankalpa - your true heart's desire - that you affirm at the start of your day.

Especially in the morning use the Sword of Nuada for protection. Especially protect yourself from the collective obsession with News broadcasting in its myriad forms with their focus on fear, separation and suffering. Intentionally switch off morning news programs. Stop being programmed. Begin to leave the Matrix that sucks the life out of you through reminding you about the unreality of separation. Walk the Beauty Way and take full responsibility for the energy you allow into your heart and mind. What you allow into your personal mind you become identified with. News programming becomes a major block to hearing the guidance from The Voice in the Stone.

> *Begin today. Declare out loud to the universe that you are willing to let go of struggle and eager to learn through joy.*
>
> ~ Sarah Ban Breathnach

Take responsibility for integration within. The word 'news' comes from combining the first letters of the four directions. This is North, East, West and South. In different traditions it is a daily practice to salute the four directions and ask for blessings of renewal. Each direction represents an aspect of yourself. The North represents battle. This is the battle inside you between the forces of separation and non-separateness. The East represents abundance and prosperity. The West represents knowledge and wisdom. The South represents music. This music is the way in which you allow the resonance of Love's Message to play through you. These aspects of you move around the centre. This centre represents your sovereignty. This is real news and invites real direction for living a life you love.

Be the King/Queen of the Palace of Presence radiating to the four directions what is central to living a meaningful and purpose filled life. This is real news. It is new and creative. It pours forth from the Cauldron of Plenty that is ever empty and forever full. This is a very different way of reading the news each day. This is news that renews you and as you broadcast invites the renewal of others. Television was intended to invite Telstar vision. I remember the Telstar 1 satellite broadcasting the first live transatlantic television feed to the sound and images of the Beatles singing, "Love, Love, Love." Real Telstar Vision is the way of seeing through the heart. Television news has dumbed down over the years into sound bites. Radio has become a series of talking heads that mirror our obsession with over-thinking. I love radio but I choose to listen to programs that invite inspiration or some form of connection to the heart.

Being Beautiful

If you find yourself unwilling to change the way you feed your personal mind you might consider that fact that news has become a form of addiction. For many people it has. Metaphorically speaking listening to a modern-day news broadcast is the equivalent of eating the poisoned apple that locks Sleeping Beauty into a deep sleep in the tower of the personal mind. This is a mind filled with words and images of separation rather than Presence. Creation created you to be a receiver of Good News. This is the news that unifies. Each day use the Sword of Nuada to ensure you stay in tune with who you are created to express. Allow yourself to expand into an open mind and into wholeheartedness. News as broadcast by the media creates fear and a feeling of lack. Use the symbolic Sword of Nuada in service of The Voice in the Stone. Start each morning with a commitment to bring a new vision of fullness to the wasteland of separateness now promoted on this planet through mainstream media..

> *Having a Vision is not enough. It must be combined with imagination, determination, faith, hope and passion. It is not enough to just stare up at the stars...we must become the stars that the stars shine down on.*
> *~ Victoria June*

Invite real Telstar vision. In this way you make time for the Timeless. You leave the slavery of *The Matrix* and begin to know you are the One. You are the One always connected to the One Life as it does Life through you. You are the One who feels the Force that turns over-thinking into miraculous thinking. Begin your day inviting the real news. Most of this journey that is The Way of Beauty is about letting go what does not serve the revelation you are created to broadcast into the world. You learn to be empty and surrendered. You commit to trusting the magnificence of the Light within and companion your greatness. You feed your mind and heart the silent soul intentions that will make you newsworthy and inspire your day for the highest good of all.

You symbolically use The Sword of Nuada to protect you from the collective forces of separateness represented by the Fir Bolg. These are the

People of the Baggage who carry the heavy burden of identification with the past and fear for the future. These are the people programmed for comfort in slavery to the separate sense of self. Through your intention you get clear and allow your heart and mind to be renewed from receiving and broadcasting the Message of Love. Start your day in this way and enter that state where you willingly invite the Universe to be expressed through you.

The day is now set up for miraculous thinking which is your being thought through. The Madman in the Cave of the Skull is now a servant to the King/Queen of Presence. You are not so anxious. You do not have to worry. You trust your ability to co-create and manifest what you need to enjoy the creative expression that is the treasure you truly are. The day moves on.

THE AFTERNOON

Each of us possesses a creative self. Claiming that is a transformational art. When you begin to act on your creativity, what you find inside may be more valuable than what you produce for the external world. The ultimate creative act is to express what is most authentic and individual about you.

- Eileen M. Clegg

Each of us will have a different structure to our day. You might be a young mother. Like myself you may be considered retired from work. You may be a motor mechanic. You might be unemployed. These different structures will present different challenges and opportunities. What is important is what you consciously intend, pay attention to and act from.

It is assumed you start your day with a conscious invitation to listening to the wisdom voice within. This is the voice within you arising from the Stillness that Speaks. You make it your conscious intention to be available to the way Love's Message speaks through you. You practice this invitation and not simply think about it. The intention to practice will bring up resistance. Expect this resistance but do not indulge such resistance. Resistance represents the battle you are engaged with. It is a battle but it need not be destructive. You can make it constructive. You can turn the lead or resistance into the gold of allowing. Metaphorically and mythological speaking you fight the Battle of Moytura. This is the battle between the forces within you identified with separateness and the forces of At-One-Ment. This, however, is only a battle from your side. The Madman in the Cave of the Skull knows he or she is fighting for control of your wild and precious life. The over-thinking personal mind will become the servant and not the dictator.

> *In the beginning it looks empty; in the end it is full, totally full, overflowing full. It is full of peace, it is full of silence, it is full of light. - Osho*

During most of the day between the early morning and late evening commit to paying attention. Invite remembrance. Invite union. One way to do this is to regularly ask, "Where am I?" This does not refer to the location you are in at the time of asking. It refers to the place you are within your consciousness. To begin with you will find for most of the time you are in your head. You are living life in words and labels. Unless you are deeply absorbed in the activity you are engaged with a conversation will be going on in your head. Usually this conversation has little or nothing to do with the present moment. Much the time this conversation is negative or judgemental in some way. You judge yourself or others.

Choose to return to the breath. Choose to feel your body and move into feeling sensational. Notice how you label everything in words. This is how most everyone lives their lives. It is a second-hand life. Life does not need you to label any experience, analyze it or compartmentalize it in words. Life happens beyond your labelling. In labelling your experience it is never fresh. It is always filtered through your experience of the past. This ties you to time and to the old.

During the day focus on feeling embodied and alert. If you do not feel much of anything start with exploring what it feels like to feel encouraged. Make it a practice to invite an experience from the Universe that allows you to feel some degree of encouragement. Do not dictate what this is. Do not grasp at something. Simply ask and be willing to receive. Stay alert but relaxed. If you worry this is a sign you are back in your personal mind and attached to your personal story.

To help you remember to ask, "Where am I?" use what I refer to as 'threshold places.' These are crossing points. It might be the door of your car. It might be the door into your place of work. It might be a door into an elevator or into a train or bus. You are moving from one clearly defined space into another. Each time choose to remember to ask the question, "Where am I?" This was the function of a now dying tradition that is the ringing the Angelus bell. The ringing of this bell served as a reminder to spread goodwill at noon each day. This is the foundation of the Islamic call to prayer. It is a call to remember to feel present to the Presence of the One Life. With prayer do not engage with more internal dialogue. Feel cantered within The Stillness that Speaks with the intention to allow that Stillness to speak through you. In this way you learn the paradoxical power of silence. This becomes your real access to power. Out of this silence you broadcast the Will to Love.

During the day pay attention to what you are broadcasting into world. You are not separate from the world although most people feel they are. Every thought, every feeling and every emotion has a different vibration. Your contribution to the health and well-being of the world is dependent on your conscious intent. If you broadcast the experience of separation this will be your experience. The Universe will simply reflect back to you the way you view the world. In my homeland of Northern Ireland the tensions within the community are reflected in the different identities that separate people into Catholics or Protestants. We see this in the Islamic world where individuals identify as Sunni Muslim or Shia Muslim. This identification with labels results in deep division, hatred and violence. The result is holy war which is anything but Holy. The real war, the real Jihad, (holy war) is happening in the personal mind of the individual. It is the Battle of Moytura happening in each moment fuelled by unconscious, obsessive over-thinking of the separate sense of self.

> *We do not create our destiny; we participate in its unfolding. Synchronicity works as a catalyst toward the working out of that destiny.*
>
> ~ David Richo

Each day be alert to synchronicity or Ah-ha moments. Such moments are confirmation the Universe is communicating through you. Synchronicity is an experience that affirms you are being guided to fulfil and embody your destiny. The personal mind will tend to dismiss these coincidences as happenstance. When such synchronistic experience happens it is important to take action to embody the message gifted through you. You might, for example, embody the invitation from meaningful co-incidence by keeping an Ah-ha journal. You write about your experience. Meaningful co-incidences tend to come in threes in quick succession. Quick succession means within a day or three. Synchronicity means you are open to miraculous thinking. This is the Universe thinking through you. This points to an increasing open energy system. You are willing to be available to The Will to Love.

To uphold this openness you need to feel anchored and relaxed in the body. The foundational way to do this is to remember to breathe correctly. The need to breathe properly cannot be overstated. During the day stop and take a slow deep conscious and refined breath. Ensure you learn to breathe in and out through the nostrils and not through the mouth. The practice of conscious breathing takes you out of The Cave of the Skull into a sense of calmness. You leave the thoughts that take you into time and separateness. You are consciously drawn into the body and become centered. Overtime this practice will lead you to a deeper sense of embodied Presence. You will begin to measure your happiness to the degree you feel the fineness of the breath. This will be a key signal about your ability to be present and feel the Presence of the One Life as it embodies you from the Unmanifest. You begin to understand the power of feeling fine.

The Way of Beauty

From this feeling of refinement you experience real peace of mind. The personal mind is still. You are going higher. You identify less with the antics of the personality. You are above the drama. You are establishing yourself in witness consciousness. The result is you feel more embodied but this is a lighter embodiment. You move away from being one of the People of the Baggage - the Fir Bolg - with their identification with the past and future. The World Health Organization (WHO) forecasts that by the year 2020 the leading cause of illness will be depression and anxiety. Depression is related to over attachment to the past while anxiety is over concern for the future.

> *The art of living... is neither careless drifting on the one hand nor fearful clinging to the past on the other. It consists in being sensitive to each moment, in regarding it as utterly new and unique, in having the mind open and wholly receptive.*
>
> *~ Alan Watts*

During the day use the Sword of Nuada and the Spear of Lugh. This is the sword of discernment. You discern through embodied awareness the flow of your energy through levels of encouragement to Essence. Follow this energy. It is not accessed through positive thinking but refined breathing and feeling sensational. In learning to feel sensational become more sensitive to your inner and outer environment. This way you pick up the subtly of Love's Message. With the Spear of Lugh focus this deepening awareness. You become one-pointed. Your awareness becomes laser like. Your focus is clear. You are now becoming one of the people with the shining brow. You are opening to seeing beyond opposites and living from unity consciousness.

THE EVENING

If you do not listen to your own original ideas, if you do not listen to your own being, you will have betrayed yourself. Also, you will have betrayed our community in failing to make your contribution to the whole.

~ Rollo May

There are two important times of the day to practice intentionality. This is at the beginning of the day when the dawn has secrets to tell you. This may not literally be at dawn but that time when you first awake. The other time is just before you go to sleep. Before going to sleep practice Yoga Nidra. In this way you program your subconscious mind and show your willingness to be available to your true heart's desire. This is your willingness to listen to The Voice in the Stone that guides your destiny. This will also improve your sleep cycle and give you deeper rest.

Yoga Nidra is the technique I use to begin and end the day. It is a body scanning technique that can last from ten minutes to forty minutes each session. To begin with listen to some Yoga Nidra recordings on Youtube that have music included with them and that guide you through the process. It is important that you choose to listen to someone whose voice you like. This is why you should listen to a few different Yoga Nidra presentations. I have made my own audio download available at

http://tonycuckson.com/yoga-nidra-guided-meditation/

During each Yoga Nidra session you are asked to state your Sankalpa. This means an intention formed by the heart's desire. Learning to discover your true heart's desire is a journey. You learn to feel what this desire is and declare it in a short phrase. The degree to which you manifest this desire will be the degree to which you feel enthusiastic. Do not be discouraged if you do not know or feel what this desire is. Try a few phrases. See how they feel. Simply make a start. Like the practice of gratitude this will be unknown but it will expand if your intention is sincere. It is important to allow this desire to arise within you rather than be dictated from the personal mind. In this way you practice the real Law of Attraction. You willingly attract through you that which is created to express through you. This is the true practice of prayer. It is following the Biblical instruction, "But when you pray, go into your room and shut the door and pray to your Father who is in secret. And your Father who sees in secret will reward you." (Matthew 6:6 E.S.V.)

The practice of Yoga Nidra is a practice of praying in secret. It is the practice of going into the inner room that is focused awareness within the body. Your Sankalpa is your statement of intent that allows Source to give through you what is best given through you. Notice here there is no reference to lack. There is no petitioning some outside force that you have to placate so you get what you ask for. Your focus is learning to receive without conditions that which is given. This is the real challenge. We direct our lives in ways we are programmed to think and feel. Happiness lies in allowing the One Life to express through an open mind and heart surrendered to Love's Purpose. This does not mean you do not use your personal mind but you use it in service of the Higher Mind which knows more than you can ever know. This is the mind that serves the inner King/Queen awake to their sovereignty.

> *You get your intuition back when you make space for it, when you stop the chattering of the rational mind.*
> —Anne Lamott

Yoga Nidra allows you to end the day in silence and focused but relaxed intentionality. This is practicing the use of all the Four Treasures of the Tuatha de Danaan at once. You enter the sleep state feeling integrated rather than distracted. In the beginning The Madman in the Cave of the Skull will return. You will learn how intense and demanding he can be. This practice is a threat to his rule over the Kingdom that is your life. Do not fight this voice in the head. Return to awareness of the breath and the body and resume the practice where you left off. This will happen much more often than you would wish. Do not allow this to discourage you. There is no success or failure here. There is only the practice. You cannot know that ten minutes intense awareness of feeling distracted does not mean that you are really awake. Over time you might do this practice for ten minutes as and when needed. One who is practiced in Yoga Nidra understands what means to pray always. To pray always is not a practice of verbalizing some demand to the Cosmos. It is the practice of being a conscious embodied receiver of Love's Message. You walk the world as the emptiness that is forever full willingly open to do the Will of Love.

Following the practice of Yoga Nidra spend time reflecting on your day unless of course you have fallen asleep. Did you feel in alignment with your morning intention? Are you grateful for what was given to you and given through you? Did you withhold Love today from anyone? Did you withhold love from yourself? Did you judge yourself or anyone else? Will you ask for forgiveness? Reflecting in this way is engaging with the task of removing blocks to Love. You do not beat yourself up if you judged or withheld love. We all do it. The more awake you become the more you will see how habitually judgement and non-loving are a major part of your everyday experience. Judgement is not discernment. Withholding love is not trusting in the emptiness that is forever full. If judgement and non-loving are the energies you focus on then these are the energies you will attract. This is the real Law of Attraction in operation.

Finally before you go to sleep intentionally ask to remember your dreams. This is the language that tells you whether your conscious and unconscious mind are in alignment. This language of dreams tells you what you need to pay attention to in order to reclaim the sovereign state of Being. Swiss psychiatrist and psychoanalyst Carl Gustav Jung said, "An unexamined dream is like an unopened letter from God." Dreams override the domination of the personal mind. They have a language beyond logic and duality. The language is symbolic, metaphoric and magical.

I invite you to learn this language of dreams. You learn this language beyond words by feeling what the symbols in the dream mean to you. Do not use dream dictionaries to interpret your dreams. Use your feelings to learn what they mean and how dreams can support you in becoming integral. In this way you honour the way in which Source energy speaks through you. Pay particular attention to recurring dreams especially any that frighten you. You may need to seek help to move beyond the fear. Dreams take you into the unknown and beyond the logical mind.

> *Dreams are illustrations...from the book your soul is writing about you."*
> *~ Marsha Norman*

In practicing Yoga Nidra - body scanning- and dream awareness you move beyond the voice in your head with which most people are obsessed. You tune into a different wavelength. You willingly allow the Universe to play a unique song and good vibration through you. You become resonant with energies that are not part of your personal agenda. You begin to invite miraculous thinking that is impersonal but Universal. The practices of Yoga Nidra and dream interpretation open the body and remove blocks to your receiving the gifts designed to come through you. This is an art to learn. It is ongoing. You do not ever arrive. There will be plateaus along the way but you can never arrive at the place you ever left. You can never leave your connection to Source energy. You are the birthless/deathless expression of Love's forever becoming.

Your choice in each moment is to listen, to trust and to companion your greatness. This is not egotism. If you are true to this invitation then the gift you become will make you humble. It comes out of a sense of amazement that what you are a part off created you to know itself through you. You know that you could never earn this magnificence. As it says in the Bible, "For what shall it profit a man, if he shall gain the whole world, and lose his own soul?" - Mark 8:36 KJV.

Being Beautiful

You might gain the whole world but if you lose your feeling connection to soul then nothing is gained. You have not known the joy of being Timeless. You have not known the joy of being deathless. You have not known the treasure that is the REAL you. Beauty is not about how you look. It is a state of Being you are and are here to Love from and as. You are already one of the Beautiful People. You are always one of the children of the Giftgiver who pours gifts through you. You are one of the Shining Brow People would that you move beyond the dualistic thinking of the personal mind and be willing to focus on heart seeing.

> *Small is the number of them that see with their own eyes and feel with their own hearts.*
> ~ Albert Einstein

In Being Beautiful you are learning one essential art. This is the art of letting go and letting be. When you fall asleep you are not doing it. Trying to go to sleep does not work. The trying keeps you awake. The Way of Beauty is the ultimate in letting go. It is awakening from the sleep of the separate sense of self. You realize yourself to be the Sleeping Beauty who was locked in the tower of the over-thinking mind. You awaken and return to earth. You are spiritually embodied. You embody Heaven on Earth and you live happily ever after. You awaken from the spell you are under and live as the treasure you are. Your joy is in pouring into the world the blessings you receive from the Giftgiver who invites union and happiness.

Conclusion

Let your light shine. Be a source of strength and courage. Share your wisdom. Radiate love.

~ Wilfred Peterson

The title of this book is *Being Beautiful*. It is not titled *Looking Beautiful*. Beauty is a state of Being. You are a Being and not a doing. Beauty is not something you do it is who you are. Beauty is a radiant aspect of the REAL you. You know you are in alignment with Love's Purpose when you broadcast the energy of beauty. In the story of The Beautiful People beauty is driven underground following the second Battle of Moytura. This is your story. Each day you are in a battle between the idea of separateness and the experience of unity.

The Way of Beauty is the way of unity and union. It is the way of the return to Kingship/Queenship and ruling from the Palace of Presence. You reclaim sovereignty from the servant who has turned the Holy Land of Ireland into a wasteland. This is a land of hungry ghosts who never feel fully nourished. There is an absence of soul. The tribe of the Fir Bolg rule this sovereign land. They carry the heavy baggage of the past and the future. They are tied to time and have lost their awareness of the Timeless.

It can be different for you. While you may not know, nor may you feel, you walk in beauty you can make the choice to explore the possibility. This is a Call to Adventure into the unknown but not the unknowable. It is an adventure in learning, not what to think, but how to think. It is learning the essential art of allowing yourself to be thought through. It is a journey from belief to beyond belief. It is a journey from ideas, concepts and labels into the awakening of insight and Knowing.

It is a most practical way of living. It is creative and expansive because it is in line with the way the Universe is designed. Rather than use seventy percent of your energy in repression of feelings use that released energy in creative expression. In this way you become openhearted and devoted. You become a devotee of the REAL you. Many of you will be at a place where you neither think nor feel beautiful. You might even consider the idea that you are beautiful to be arrogant. Rather I invite you to consider this as an invitation to freedom.

> *Once you choose to love yourself and align with your Spirit, life aligns with you.*
>
> *- Sonia Choquette, The Answer is Simple...Love Yourself, Live Your Spirit!*

You are here to be a beautiful and fulfilled expression of Love's Purpose. Trust me when I say this is your joy. You pour your life energy forth from this feeling connection to Source. Beauty becomes you but it is a reflection of the beauty of the Giftgiver in whose image you are made. The word 'made' is not really the right word. It suggests you are a mechanism rather than an energetic happening. You are more a flow, a verb, rather than a thing, rather than a noun. Remember beauty is a state of Being. It is a state you learn to allow. It is an art you develop over time so you enter the Timeless.

This needs commitment, discipline and practice. Without practice The Way of Beauty is simply an idea. It is merely more information. It does not become a vehicle for transformation. The practices are practices of paradox. You are practicing non-achievement. You are practicing letting go. You are practicing non-judgement. In this way you learn how to descend into the emptiness that is forever full. This requires trust and faith that the Universe has your back. This trust and faith is developed through experience and not through cerebral belief. You are attending at a real university. This is the

Conclusion

school of Love that verses you in unknowing and sets you on fire. This is a university education that allows you to know the truth of who you are.

Education is not the filling of a pail but the lighting of a fire.
– W.B. Yeats

This key focus is learning how to feel your connection to the Universe and allow that Universe to express through you. You are invited to allow Heaven to be on Earth. You practice The Lasting Privilege which is to be a channel of Love. In so allowing you will know what it is to feel the Presence of beauty that is your natural state of Being.

Your foundational practice is learning to feel fine through connection to conscious breathing. Another foundational practice is to feel sensational. Spend more time being present to the body. This is the whole body and not just the inside of your head. As a result you will begin to feel meditative and centered for no reason. Reason is no longer running the whole show. The Madman in the Cave of the Skull has become the servant. He or she comes when you intend to use the gift of the rational mind. The rational mind serves the Message of Love as it flows through an open-heart and mind.

The story of *The Four Treasures of the Tuatha de Danaan* shows you the treasures you are to claim. This story invites you to make these treasures key to how you intend to uniquely express sovereignty. This is the sovereignty designed to reign through you. In this way you create an inner land of blessings and abundance that you then broadcast into the world. Your first task is to listen to The Voice in the Stone which is your personal Y.E.S. To listen you have to be silent.

Be silent now. Say fewer and fewer love poems. Let yourself become living poetry. - Rumi.

To be silent is a great challenge in today's world. Silence appears at first to be nothing. There are so many other things to do. To live as the beauty you are learn how to allow and do nothing. Explore what it feels like to get out of the way and allow the magnificence of who you are to be known. For many, even most people, this is a turnaround in the way they focus their energy. All wisdom teachers from all traditions invite this journey of dying into Life. The less there is of you as the personal mind the more there is available to you of the miraculous Mind. No need to worry. There is no loss here. The guide you have is unconditional Love would that you trust this.

The time to begin to trust this Universal Gift giving is now. Timeless beauty is not reflected in the pages of glossy magazines with Photoshop images of beautiful looking people. You reveal the Beauty you are. Yours is the story of The Ugly Duckling looking in the clear waters of Universal Mind and seeing (knowing) itself as a Being of grace and beauty. This was always the destiny of The Ugly Duckling beyond its birth into the farmyard that represents The Ordinary World of everyday living. This is your destiny to be expressed through you in a unique way.

You are the one who is to journey to The Lake of Revelation. This is the journey of the open mind and heart willing to listen to The Voice in the Stone. This is The Still Small Voice flowing through a body that is less armoured by fear of feeling. You go to The Lake of Revelation and you know you are made in the image of the Giftgiver. You come home to the Promised Land. You want one thing. Your heart's desire, metaphorically speaking, is to return to Egypt to free the chosen people from the slavery to the idea of the separate sense of self. We are all chosen otherwise you would not be here on this planet. It is my hope that you now commit to allowing the revelation that is the treasure you are. Let it be so for you. Let it be so for all.

Bibliography

1. **Benner, Joseph.** *The Impersonal Life.* s.l.: Devorss & Co, June 1, 1941.
2. **Peace, Foundation for Inner.** *A Course in Miracles.* s.l.: Foundation for Inner Peace, 1975.
3. **Waterboys, The.** World Party. *Fisherman's Blues.* [CD] s.l.: Parlaphone, 2016.
4. **Cuckson, Tony.** *Awakening the Heart - 21 Ways to Follow Love's Message.* Dowra, Co. Cavan: The Yeats Experience Academy, 2016.
5. **Masters, Robert Augustus .** *Spiritual Bypassing - When Spirituality Disconnects Us from What Really Matters.* s.l: North Atlantic Books, July 27, 2010.
6. **Joyce, James.** *Dubliners.* s.l. : Prestwick House, Inc, September 1st, 2006.
7. **Tipping, Colin.** *Radical Forgiveness - A Revolutionary Five Stage Process to Heal Relationships.* s.l. : Sounds True, January 1st 2010.
8. **Zwig, Connie.** *The Holy Longing - The Hidden Power of Spiritual Yearning.* s.l.: TarcherPerigee, February 10, 2003.
9. **Thrine, Ralph Waldo.** *In Tune With the Infinite.* s.l. : Wilder Publications, May 6, 2008.
10. **Dürckheim, Karlfried Graf.** *Hara - The Vital Centre of Man.* s.l. : Inner Traditions; 4 edition, October 27, 2004.

INDEX

2

21 Ways to Follow Love's Message · 11, 154

A

A Course in Miracles · 4, 44
Abraham Maslow · 12
ADD and ADHD · 15
affirmations · 30
Ah-ha moments · 136
Alan Watts · 137
Albert Einstein · 5, 14, 142
Amergin Glúingel · 76
Anam Cara · 40, 111
Angelus bell · 135
Anne Lamott · 139
Anthon St. Maarten · 37
Antonio Machado · 91
Aristotle · 116
armored by judgments · 36
atheist of agnostic · 17
Awakening the Heart · 154
awareness watching awareness · 99

B

Baba Yaga · 79
Banba, Ériu and Fódla · 76
Battle of Moytura · 57, 58, 87, 95, 134, 136, 143
Beatles · 43, 131
Beauty and the Beast · 79

Beginners Mind · 101
Bill Donohue · 34
Bob Marley · 108
Bodhisattva · 18
body armor · 29
body scan · 128
Breakthrough Experience · 73, 115
Brer Rabbit · 15
Buddha · 96, 115
Buddhism · 18, 28

C

Call to Adventure · 66, 72, 80, 86
Carl Gustav Jung · 140
Caroline Myss PhD · 29
Cauldron of Plenty · 36, 63, 83, 85, 112, 116
character armor · 31
Christ consciousness · 21
Cinderella · x
cognitive enlightenment · 30
Colin Tipping · 30
collective consciousness · 42
collective unconscious · 24, 127
companion your greatness · 48, 51
Connie Zweig · 30
conscious belly breathing · 96
conscious breathing · 136
conscious mind · 18
couch potato · 27

D

Dalai Lama · 112
Daniel LaRusso · 97
David Augsberger · 7

Index

David Whyte · 29
Deepak Chopra · 107, 122
depression and anxiety · 137
Derek Walcott · 89
desert of unknowing · 41
detachment from feelings · 35, 110
devotional singing · 33
discernment · 82, 104, 137, 140
Doc Childre · 125
dream interpretation · 141
dualistic thinking · 88, 142

E

Eckhart Tolle · 97
Eire - Ireland · 76
emotional and feeling life · 27
emotional splurging · 31
energetic transmission · 63
energy body · 47
energy of manifestation · 48
eternal life · 61

F

Facebook · 15
fairy stories · 60
fairy tales · 23, 79
Falias, Gorias, Murias and Finias · 74
field of awareness · 45
Fir Bolg · 57, 86, 87, 132, 137, 143
fire and the hearth · 53
Flight of the Jews · 17
Friends of the Western Buddhist Order (FWBO) · 28, 45

G

Garden of Eden · 28
Gary Zukav · 119
Georges Gurdjieff · xi
Good God Dadga · 85
good vibration · 25, 63, 125

H

Hans Christian Andersen · 13
happily ever after · 60
happy for no reason · 38, 45, 74, 99
Hecate · 79
higher economic growth · 69
higher feelings · 31, 120
Higher Mind · 25, 139
holons · 25
Holy Land of Ireland · 9, 86
home frequency · 5
hungry ghosts · 143

I

illusion of separation · 111
Infinite Field of Intention · 81
inner guidance · 88
inner guidance system · 29
inner knowing. · 5
inner seeing and Knowing · 43
inner witness · 103
insight and revelation · 59
intention and attention · 68
internal guidance system · 35
Islamic call to prayer · 135

J

James Joyce · 28
Japanese poet Basho · 44
Jeddu Krishnamurti · 9, 19
Jerry Maguire · 16
Jihad · 104, 135
Johann Wolfgang von Goethe · 113, 116
John O'Donohue · 111
Jonathan H. Ellerby · 98
Joseph Bremer · xi
Judgement Day · 104

K

Kahlil Gibran · viii, 117
Kali · 79
Karlfried Graf Dürckheim · 97
Karmic consequences · 104
Kensuke Miyagi · 97
Khalil Gibran · 118
Kirtan · 33, 129
Knowing Mind · 23
Krishna Consciousness (ISKCON) · 28

L

Lake of Revelation · 71, 146
Land of Promise · 74
Land of the Forever Young · 70
Law of Attraction · 42, 43, 50, 69
Law of Karma · 104
levels of mind · 25
logic chopping · 52
Lord of the Dance · 126
Luke Skywalker · 80, 113

M

magical thinking · 42, 43
Margaret J. Wheatley · 95
Mary Oliver · 53
Matthew Fox · 107
Max Ehrmann · 81
meditation, prayer or contemplation · 100
Meister Eckhart · 11, 14, 81
metaphysical story · 17
Mike Scott · 7
Mind of Christ · 9, 21, 69
mindfulness · 114
miraculous thinking · 38, 42, 50, 132, 133, 136, 141
Moses · 17
mythological stories · 52

N

Neil Anderson (Son of Man · 91
Northern Ireland · 20, 67, 108, 135
Nowhere Man · 43

O

Obi-Wan Kenobi · 80, 113
observation and detachment · 71
One Mind · 62, 63
Oprah Winfrey · 105
original face · 113
Osho · 23, 52, 94, 134
over-thinking · 43, 64, 82

P

Palace of Presence · 80, 82, 131, 143
Pandora's Box · 48
paralysis by analysis · 30
Paulo Coelho · 82, 112
peace activism · 24
peace of mind · 41, 97
Penney Peirce · 5
People of the Baggage · 96
personal empowerment · 37, 39
Pharaoh · 17, 24
Photoshop images · 146
positive thinking · 9, 30, 33, 47
practice of meditation · 101
Primary Intention · 62
Prodigal Son · 4, 71
Promised Land · 17, 23
Purpose of Love · 62

R

radiant inter-dependence · 62
Ralph Waldo Trine · 64
rational mind · 45
real university education · 101
Red Sea · 17

Index

Refusal of the Call · 72
relationship of co-dependence · 62
René Descartes · 14
Renée Zellweger · 16
return to Egypt · 18
Richard Rohr · 19
Road of Trials · 73
Robert Augustus Masters, PhD · 27
Rollo May · 138
Russian folktale · 79

S

Sangharakshita · 28
Sankalpa · 107, 129, 130, 138, 139
Sarah Ban Breathnach · 123, 131
Satori · 115
Secret of Secrets · 37, 43, 58
self-actualization · 12
Shia Muslim · 135
shifting sands of time · 49
Shining Brow People · 142
Sigmund Freud · 96
silent witnessing · 104
Simon and Garfunkel · 109
Slavic folklore · 79
Sleeping Beauty · x, 4, 43, 79, 90, 92, 118, 142
Snow White · 71, 92
Sonia Choquette · 144
soul awareness · 36
Sounds True · 107
Spear of Lugh · 74, 83, 110, 112
Spiritual Bypassing · 28
Sri Chinmoy · 93
St. Paul · 9
Star Wars · 80, 113
Still Small Voice · 95
Stone of Destiny · 53, 80, 97, 102
storytelling trance · 52
Stradivarius · 7
subconscious mind · 59, 138
Sunni Muslim · 135
Sword of Nuada · 81, 107
synchronicity · 136

T

Tar Baby Experience · 15
Telstar 1 satellite · 131
The Boon Tree · 107
The Catholic League · 34
The Cauldron of Plenty · 9, 74
The Cloud of Unknowing · 23, 73
The Emperor's New Clothes · 13
The Giftgiver · 39, 54, 64, 67
The Hero's Journey · 72
the holy instant · 4, 44
The Holy Land · 77
The Karate Kid · 97
The Lasting Privilege · 145
The Matrix · xi, 71, 91, 111
The Ordinary World · 73
The People of the Shining Brow · 64, 66
The Promised Land · 77
The Secret · 43
The Shining Ones · 64
The Stone of Destiny · 74
The Voyage and Return · 109
The War on Terror · 15
The Waterboys · 7
The Wishing Tree · 107
The World Health Organization (WHO) · 137
theory of mind · 25
Thích Nhất Hạnh · 114
threshold of consciousness · 99
time poverty · 17
Tir Na Nog · 70
Tom Cruise · 16
Tony Robbins · 110
transatlantic television · 131
transmission of Knowing · 52
Tree of Good and Evil · 28

U

Ugly Duckling · 71, 98
unconscious mind · 140
United Kingdom · 108
unity consciousness · 137

universal intelligence · 10
Universal Mind · 7, 9, 11, 23
Unknowing Mind · 19

V

Vasilisa the Beautiful · 79
Vipassana Meditation · 28
vision board · 43
Voice in the Stone · 80, 82, 88
voice in your head · 71

W

W. B. Yeats · 6, 8, 26, 64, 77, 78, 158
W. Clement Stone · 121
Wandering Aengus · 6, 64, 65, 66
Way of Beauty · 96

Wayne Dyer · 83
Wilhelm Reich · 29
Will to Love · 83
William Anthony "Bill" Donohue · 34
William Blake · 17
William Wordsworth · 77
witness consciousness · 71, 83, 110, 137

Y

Yoga · 4
Yoga Nidra · 101, 128, 138, 140, 141
Youtube · 138

Z

Zen Master · 36

Other Books

AWAKENING THE HEART

Overall this is a beautiful book for anyone feeling the call to the heart.

-Eliza Erikson - Woman's Energetics - Healing the Subtle Body

The quality of your life depends on one essential ingredient. This is the degree to which you can give and receive love. Every day, in every way, the Message of Love is speaking to you to be uniquely and gloriously expressed through you. You are designed to be a unique and radiant expression of Love in form.

Being Beautiful

Awakening the Heart – 21 Ways to Follow Love's Message shares twenty-one ways to become aware that Love is a state of Being that you are each and every day. Healing the Heart Chakra is about who you are at the very centre of your Being. Healing the heart chakra is not about finding love but dissolving all the blocks that keep you from your essential nature as Love's radiant presence expressing its fullness through you.

In this compelling, beautiful and practical book you are invited to begin from a profound understanding. This is the realization that you are Love and are being informed by the radiance of Love in each and every moment. When you are in alignment with this essential wisdom, then you become the fulfilled. You open the heart to the fullness you are created to be, expand into and to pour away in glory for the highest good of all. In both profound and practical ways, this book shows you ways to open the heart center through awareness of your everyday life experience. This includes becoming aware of the way in which the Message of Love speaks to you through the songs you sing or listen to, the movies you watch and books you read. You are invited to realize peace of mind and be in touch with that which is sensational within you.

In whatever way love manifests in your life at this time, Healing the Heart Chakra will help you see your journey in a wonderfully heroic way and allow you to live everyday with greater joy and fulfillment. The Message of Love will be realized as your very essence and you will radiate your light into the world with power, presence and beauty. You will realize that you really are a star in the making. Such is the invitation from Awakening the Heart - 21 Ways to Follow Love's Message.

Print books and Kindle formats available at Amazon

EBook available for download here

https://www.smashwords.com/books/view/463842

Other Books

AWAKENING TO LOVE

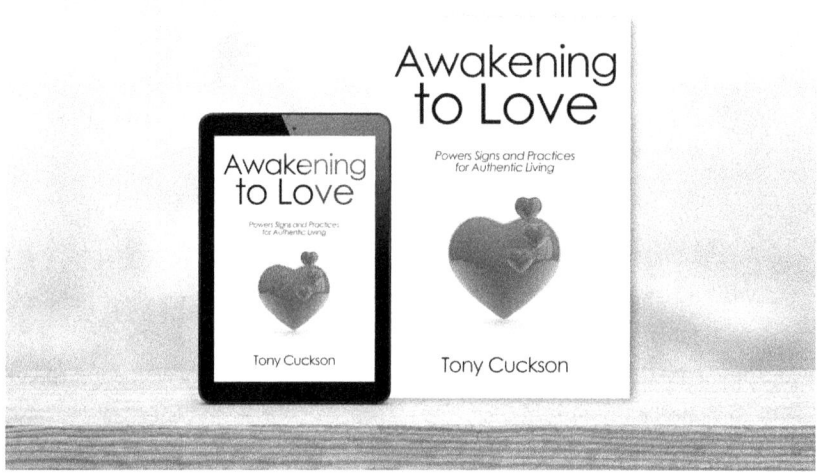

Your task is not to seek for love, but merely to seek and find all the barriers within yourself that you have built against it.

- *Rumi*

Very few people have learned to love themselves. They have never been shown what healthy self-love and self-care look and feel like. The result is unhealthy dependence on others, food, alcohol or drugs and increasingly on media and technology.

In Awakening to Love you'll discover powers and signs for living an authentic life and feeling a deeper connection with the Divine within. Learn practices that dissolve limiting modes of thought, and create real happiness, success, authentic self-expression and love. This includes:-

Learning the one practice worth a year's workshop training that is in front of your very nose.

Follow a daily awakening program for morning, afternoon and evening to fit your busy schedule.

Deepen soul mate love through discovering and celebrating your most authentic self.

Live the strangest paradox that will free to you Love who you truly are and live a life you love.

Awakening to Love includes a guided meditation to invite you to access the wisdom of the body and innate inner guidance system. Take the longest shortest journey and most empowering journey of your life. This is the journey from the head to the heart. Step onto the path of Awakening to Love and companion your greatness.

EBook Download available here

https://www.smashwords.com/books/view/757352

ABOUT THE AUTHOR

The only sane thing a man can do is give Love - Hafiz

I write about what I long to discover, re-member and invite. I long to re-member what it feels to experience union. This is union of the human with the Divine, time with Eternity and the finite with the Infinite. This is union that brings true fulfillment and finds deep fulfillment in pouring healing into the world for the highest good of all.

Being Beautiful

The books I write, the songs I sing, the stories I tell arise from a personal journey of prayer, meditation, contemplation and self-discovery. Writing them, singing them and telling them is both a joy and a challenge. These are written with the intention of pointing a way toward revelation and, in the words of W. B. Yeats from his poem *These are the Clouds,* invite you to "companion your greatness."

It is my wish that *Being Beautiful – Learning to Treasure the REAL You* allows you to feel and celebrate your unique connection to the Source of the One Life that is true fulfillment. In this way I fulfill the invitation from my beloved poet Hafiz of Shiraz when he invites:-

> Why not become one who lives with a full moon in each eye
> Speaking that sweet moon language
> That every other eye in the world is longing to hear.

May this book help light your way through the darkness of the separate sense of the suffering self to the enlightened revelation that you magnificently are.

Connect with Tony

Website and Blog http://www.tonycuckson.com
Twitter: http://www.twitter.com/tonycuckson
Facebook: http://www.facebook.com/tonycuckson
Email:- storyteller@tonycuckson.com

www.ingramcontent.com/pod-product-compliance
Lightning Source LLC
LaVergne TN
LVHW051601070426
835507LV00021B/2693